Easy and Affordable Air Fryer Cookbook UK

1800 Days of Healthy Affordable Air Fry Over Recipes Using European Measurement Units for Cooking

Amanda A. Harper

CONTENTS

Poultry Recipes 41

Fish & Seafood Recipes 52

Vegetarian & Vegan Recipes 62

Side Dishes Recipes **73**

Introduction

In recent years, the kitchen landscape has seen a revolutionary addition that has transformed the way we cook - the air fryer. With its promise of healthier, quicker, and more convenient cooking, the air fryer has become a beloved kitchen appliance for many households around the world. If you're new to the world of air fryers or looking to master your skills, you've come to the right place. In this comprehensive guide, we'll take you on a journey through the world of air fryers, from understanding how they work to mastering the art of cooking in them, and finally, ensuring their longevity through proper cleaning and maintenance.

What is an Air Fryer?

Understanding the Technology

At its core, an air fryer is a kitchen appliance that cooks food by circulating hot air around it. It achieves a similar crispiness to traditional frying but with a fraction of the oil or even no oil at all. The magic behind this cooking method lies in the appliance's ability to rapidly heat and circulate air, creating a crispy outer layer while keeping the inside tender and moist. This process is what makes air fryers a game-changer in the culinary world.

Why Choose an Air Fryer?

Healthier Cooking: One of the primary reasons people turn to air fryers is the reduced need for oil. You can enjoy your favorite fried foods with significantly less fat and calories, making it a healthier choice for your diet.

Time Efficiency: Air fryers preheat quickly and cook food faster than traditional ovens. This means you can prepare meals in a fraction of the time, making it a great option for busy individuals and families.

Versatility: Air fryers are not limited to just frying. They can also bake, roast, grill, and even reheat leftovers effectively, making them a versatile addition to your kitchen.

Easy Cleanup: With less oil involved, cleaning up after cooking with an air fryer is a breeze. Most parts are dishwasher safe, saving you time and effort.

Less Odor: Compared to deep frying, air frying produces fewer cooking odors, making it a more pleasant experience in your kitchen.

Getting Started with Your Air Fryer

2Unboxing and Setup

When you bring home a new air fryer, the excitement of healthier cooking possibilities awaits. Here's a step-by-step guide to help you get started:

Unboxing: Carefully unpack your air fryer and inspect all the components, including the cooking basket, tray, and any included accessories. Read the user manual thoroughly to familiarize yourself with your specific model.

Placement: Choose a suitable location in your kitchen for your air fryer. Ensure it has enough space around it for proper ventilation and safe operation. Avoid placing it near walls or cabinets that might obstruct airflow.

Preparation: Wash all removable parts, including the cooking basket and tray, with warm, soapy water. Dry them thoroughly before use.

Preheating: Preheat your air fryer according to the manufacturer's instructions. Preheating ensures even cooking and optimal results.

Basic Operation

Now that your air fryer is ready to go, let's explore its basic operation:

Loading the Basket: Place the food you wish to cook in the cooking basket. It's essential not to overcrowd the basket, as this can hinder air circulation and result in uneven cooking.

Setting the Temperature: Select the desired cooking temperature using the control panel. Most air fryers allow you to adjust the temperature between 300°F (149°C) and 400°F (204°C), but check your specific model for its range.

Setting the Time: Set the cooking time using the timer function. Air fryers typically have a timer that can be set for up to 60 minutes. Keep an eye on the cooking progress, especially if you're trying a new recipe.

Cooking: Once you've set the temperature and time, start the air fryer. The hot air will circulate around the food, cooking it to perfection. You may need to shake or flip the food halfway through the cooking time for even results.

Tips for Successful Air Frying

While air fryers are relatively straightforward to use, here are some tips to ensure your dishes come out perfectly:

Use the Right Amount of Oil: While air fryers use significantly less oil than traditional frying, a light coating of oil on your food can enhance the crispiness. You can use a spray bottle to apply a fine mist of oil or invest in an oil sprayer for more precise control.

Don't Overcrowd the Basket: To achieve the best results, leave enough space between food items in the cooking basket. Overcrowding can lead to uneven cooking and less crispy results.

Shake or Flip: For even cooking, shake or flip your food halfway through the cooking time. This helps ensure that all sides are exposed to the hot air.

Use Parchment Paper or Liners: To simplify cleanup and prevent sticking, consider using parchment paper or silicone liners in the cooking basket. Be sure to check if your specific air fryer model allows for this.

Monitor the Cooking: Keep an eye on your food, especially the first few times you use your air fryer. Cooking times may vary depending on the model and the type of food you're preparing.

Preheat When Necessary: While not all recipes require preheating, some benefit from a few minutes of preheating to ensure consistent results. Check your recipe for guidance.

Air Fryer Recipes and Cooking Techniques

Cooking a Variety of Foods

Air fryers are incredibly versatile and can handle a wide range of dishes. Here are some popular foods you can prepare in your air fryer:

French Fries: Achieve crispy, golden fries with just a fraction of the oil compared to deep frying.

Chicken Wings: Make restaurant-quality wings with perfectly crispy skin and tender meat.

Vegetables: Roast your favorite veggies with a drizzle of oil and your choice of seasonings.

Fish: Enjoy flaky, flavorful fish fillets with a crispy exterior.

Burgers and Sandwiches: Cook juicy burgers or grilled sandwiches with ease.

Frozen Foods: Air fryers are excellent for reheating and crisping up frozen foods like pizza, chicken nuggets, and mozzarella sticks.

Cooking Techniques

Different cooking techniques can be employed with your air fryer, allowing you to experiment with various flavors and textures:

Baking: Bake cookies, muffins, and even small cakes in your air fryer for quick, individual-sized treats.

Grilling: Achieve grill marks and a smoky flavor by using the grill pan accessory included with some air fryer models.

Roasting: Roast vegetables, meats, or even whole chickens for a savory, oven-baked taste.

Dehydrating: Some air fryers have a dehydrating function, which is perfect for making homemade dried fruits, beef jerky, or crispy kale chips.

Reheating: Reheat leftovers with the air fryer to maintain their crispy texture rather than using the microwave.

Cleaning and Maintenance

Cleaning Your Air Fryer

Proper cleaning is essential to maintain the performance and longevity of your air fryer. Here's a step-by-step guide:

Cool Down: Always ensure your air fryer has cooled down before cleaning. The components can be extremely hot immediately after cooking.

Unplug the Appliance: For safety reasons, unplug the air fryer before you begin cleaning.

Remove and Clean Removable Parts: Take out the cooking basket, tray, and any other removable components. Wash them with warm, soapy water. Most air fryer accessories are dishwasher safe, but check your user manual to be sure.

Wipe Down the Interior: Use a damp cloth or sponge to wipe down the interior of the air fryer. Be careful not to scratch any non-stick surfaces.

Clean the Heating Element: If your air fryer has a visible heating element, clean it carefully with a soft brush or cloth to remove any residue.

Exterior Cleaning: Wipe the exterior of the air fryer with a damp cloth to remove any grease or food splatters.

Empty the Crumb Tray: If your air fryer has a crumb tray, remove it, and discard any accumulated crumbs or debris.

Dry Thoroughly: Ensure all parts are completely dry before reassembling and using your air fryer again.

Maintenance Tips

To keep your air fryer in excellent working condition, consider these maintenance tips:

Regularly Inspect for Wear and Tear: Check your air fryer's power cord, plug, and any other components for signs of damage. If you notice any issues, contact the manufacturer for repairs or replacements.

Oil the Moving Parts: Some air fryers have moving parts that may benefit from occasional oiling to prevent rust or friction. Refer to your user manual for guidance on lubrication.

Replace Parts as Needed: Over time, some parts like filters or heating elements may wear out. Replace these parts as recommended by the manufacturer to maintain optimal performance.

Store Properly: When not in use, store your air fryer in a cool, dry place away from direct sunlight and moisture.

Breakfast & Snacks And Fries Recipes

Morning Sausage Wraps

Servings: 8

Ingredients:

- 8 sausages, chopped into pieces
- 2 slices of cheddar cheese, cut into quarters
- 1 can of regular crescent roll dough
- 8 wooden skewers

Directions:

1. Take the dough and separate each one
2. Cut open the sausages evenly
3. The one of your crescent rolls and on the widest part, add a little sausage and then a little cheese
4. Roll the dough and tuck it until you form a triangle
5. Repeat this for four times and add into your air fryer
6. Cook at 190ºC for 3 minutes
7. Remove your dough and add a skewer for serving
8. Repeat with the other four pieces of dough

Breakfast Doughnuts

Servings: 4

Ingredients:

- 1 packet of Pillsbury Grands
- 5 tbsp raspberry jam
- 1 tbsp melted butter
- 5 tbsp sugar

Directions:

1. Preheat your air fryer to 250ºC
2. Place the Pillsbury Grands into the air fryer and cook for around 5m minutes
3. Remove and place to one side
4. Take a large bowl and add the sugar
5. Coat the doughnuts in the melted butter, coating evenly
6. Dip into the sugar and coat evenly once more
7. Using an icing bag, add the jam into the bag and pipe an even amount into each doughnut
8. Eat warm or cold

Healthy Stuffed Peppers

Servings: 2

Ingredients:

- 1 large bell pepper, deseeded and cut into halves
- 1 tsp olive oil
- 4 large eggs
- Salt and pepper to taste

Directions:

1. Take your peppers and rub a little olive oil on the edges
2. Into each pepper, crack one egg and season with salt and pepper
3. You will need to insert a trivet into your air fryer to hold the peppers, and then arrange the peppers evenly
4. Set your fryer to 200°C and cook for 13 minutes
5. Once cooked, remove and serve with a little more seasoning, if required

Tangy Breakfast Hash

Servings: 6

Ingredients:

- 2 tbsp olive oil
- 2 sweet potatoes, cut into cubes
- 1 tbsp smoked paprika
- 1 tsp salt
- 1 tsp black pepper
- 2 slices of bacon, cut into small pieces

Directions:

1. Preheat your air fryer to 200°C
2. Pour the olive oil into a large mixing bowl
3. Add the bacon, seasonings, potatoes and toss to evenly coat
4. Transfer the mixture into the air fryer and cook for 12-16 minutes
5. Stir after 10 minutes and continue to stir periodically for another 5 minutes

Loaded Hash Browns

Servings: 4

Ingredients:

- 4 large potatoes
- 2 tbsp bicarbonate of soda
- 1 tbsp salt
- 1 tbsp black pepper
- 1 tsp cayenne pepper
- 2 tbsp olive oil
- 1 large chopped onion
- 1 chopped red pepper
- 1 chopped green pepper

Directions:

1. Grate the potatoes
2. Squeeze out any water contained within the potatoes
3. Take a large bowl of water and add the potatoes
4. Add the bicarbonate of soda, combine everything and leave to soak for 25 minutes
5. Drain the water away and carefully pat the potatoes to dry
6. Transfer your potatoes into another bowl
7. Add the spices and oil
8. Combining everything well, tossing to coat evenly
9. Place your potatoes into your fryer basket
10. Set to 200°C and cook for 10 minutes
11. Give the potatoes a shake and add the peppers and the onions
12. Cook for another 10 minutes

Easy Air Fryer Sausage

Servings: 5

Ingredients:

- 5 uncooked sausages
- 1 tbsp mustard
- Salt and pepper for seasoning

Directions:

1. Line the basket of your fryer with parchment paper
2. Arrange the sausages inside the basket
3. Set to 180°C and cook for 15 minutes
4. Turn the sausages over and cook for another 5 minutes
5. Remove and cool
6. Drizzle the mustard over the top and season to your liking

Breakfast "pop Tarts"

Servings: 6

Ingredients:

- 2 slices of prepared pie crust, shortbread or filo will work fine
- 2 tbsp strawberry jam
- 60ml plain yogurt
- 1 tsp cornstarch
- 1 tsp Stevia sweetener
- 2 tbsp cream cheese
- A drizzle of olive oil

Directions:

1. Lay your pie crust flat and cut into 6 separate rectangular pieces
2. In a small bowl, mix together the cornstarch and the jam
3. Spread 1 tablespoon of the mixture on top of the crust
4. Fold each crust over to form the tart
5. Seal down the edges using a fork
6. Arrange your tarts inside the frying basket and spray with a little olive oil
7. Heat to 175°C and cook for 10 minutes
8. Meanwhile, combine the yogurt, cream cheese and Stevia in a bowl
9. Remove the tarts and allow to cool
10. Once cool, add the frosting on top and sprinkle with the sugar sprinkles

Crunchy Mexican Breakfast Wrap

Servings: 2

Ingredients:

- 2 large tortillas
- 2 corn tortillas
- 1 sliced jalapeño pepper
- 4 tbsp ranchero sauce
- 1 sliced avocado
- 25g cooked pinto beans

Directions:

1. Take each of your large tortillas and add the egg, jalapeño, sauce, the corn tortillas, the avocado and the pinto beans, in that order. If you want to add more sauce at this point, you can
2. Fold over your wrap to make sure that nothing escapes
3. Place each wrap into your fryer and cook at 190°C for 6 minutes
4. Remove your wraps and place in the oven, cooking for a further 5 minutes at 180°C, until crispy
5. Place each wrap into a frying pan and crisp a little more on a low heat, for a couple of minutes on each side

Mexican Breakfast Burritos

Servings: 6

Ingredients:

- 6 scrambled eggs
- 6 medium tortillas
- Half a minced red pepper
- 8 sausages, cut into cubes and browned
- 4 pieces of bacon, pre-cooked and cut into pieces
- 65g grated cheese of your choice
- A small amount of olive oil for cooking

Directions:

1. Into a regular mixing bowl, combine the eggs, bell pepper, bacon pieces, the cheese, and the browned sausage, giving everything a good stir
2. Take your first tortilla and place half a cup of the mixture into the middle, folding up the top and bottom and rolling closed
3. Repeat until all your tortillas have been used
4. Arrange the burritos into the bottom of your fryer and spray with a little oil
5. Cook the burritos at 170°C for 5 minutes

Easy Cheesy Scrambled Eggs

Servings: 1

Ingredients:

- 1 tbsp butter
- 2 eggs
- 100g grated cheese
- 2 tbsp milk
- Salt and pepper for seasoning

Directions:

1. Add the butter inside the air fryer pan and cook at 220ºC until the butter has melted
2. Add the eggs and milk to a bowl and combine, seasoning to your liking
3. Pour the eggs into the butter panned cook for 3 minutes, stirring around lightly to scramble
4. Add the cheese and cook for another 2 more minutes

Apple Crisps

Servings: 2

Ingredients:

- 2 apples, chopped
- 1 tsp cinnamon
- 2 tbsp brown sugar
- 1 tsp lemon juice
- 2.5 tbsp plain flour
- 3 tbsp oats
- 2 tbsp cold butter
- Pinch of salt

Directions:

1. Preheat the air fryer to 260ºC
2. Take a 5" baking dish and crease
3. Take a large bowl and combine the apples with the sugar, cinnamon and lemon juice
4. Add the mixture to the baking dish and cover with aluminium foil
5. Place in the air fryer and cook for 15 minutes
6. Open the lid and cook for another 5 minutes
7. Combine the rest of the ingredients in a food processor, until a crumble-type mixture occurs
8. Add over the top of the cooked apples
9. Cook with the lid open for another 5 minutes
10. Allow to cool a little before serving

Meaty Egg Cups

Servings: 4

Ingredients:

- 8 slices of toasted sandwich bread
- 2 slices of ham
- 4 eggs
- Salt and pepper to taste
- Butter for greasing

Directions:

1. Take 4 ramekins and grease the insides with a little butter
2. Flatten the slices of toast with a rolling pin and arrange inside the ramekins - two in each
3. Line the inside of each ramekin with a slice of ham
4. Crack one egg into each ramekin
5. Season with a little salt and pepper
6. Place the ramekins into the air fryer and cook at 160°C for 15 minutes
7. Remove from the fryer and wait to cool just slightly
8. Remove and serve

Sauces & Snack And Appetiser Recipes

Air Fryer Turkey Melt Sandwich

Servings: 1

Cooking Time: 10 Mints

Ingredients:

- 2 slices bread
- Slices leftover turkey slices or deli meat
- 1 Tablespoon butter
- good melting cheese (American, Swiss, cheddar, Gruyere, etc.)

Directions:

1. Layer cheese and turkey slices in between bread. Butter outside of bread with butter. Secure the top slice of bread with toothpicks through the sandwich. Lay sandwich in an air fryer basket.
2. Air Fry at 360°F/180°C for about 3-5 minutes to melt the cheese.
3. Flip the sandwich and increase heat to 380°F/190°C to finish and crisp the bread. Air Fry at 380°F/190°C for about 5 minutes or until the sandwich is to your preferred texture. Check on the sandwich often to make sure it doesn't burn. Allow it to cool a bit before biting into the yummy grilled cheese sandwich

Pretzel Bites

Servings: 2

Ingredients:

- 650g flour
- 2.5 tsp active dry yeast
- 260ml hot water
- 1 tsp salt
- 4 tbsp melted butter
- 2 tbsp sugar

Directions:

1. Take a large bowl and add the flour, sugar and salt
2. Take another bowl and combine the hot water and yeast, stirring until the yeast has dissolved
3. Then, add the yeast mixture to the flour mixture and use your hands to combine
4. Knead for 2 minutes
5. Cover the bowl with a kitchen towel for around half an hour
6. Divide the dough into 6 pieces
7. Preheat the air fryer to 260°C
8. Take each section of dough and tear off a piece, rolling it in your hands to create a rope shape, that is around 1" in thickness
9. Cut into 2" strips
10. Place the small dough balls into the air fryer and leave a little space in-between
11. Cook for 6 minutes
12. Once cooked, remove and brush with melted butter and sprinkle salt on top

Air Fryer Pizza Scrolls Recipe

Servings: 2

Cooking Time: 10 Mints

Ingredients:

- 1/2 of a portion of pizza dough recipe
- 2 portions of roasted tomato pizza sauce
- 60 g grated mozzarella and cheddar mix
- Mixed Italian herbs

Directions:

1. Roll out the pizza dough.
2. Spread over the tomato pizza sauce.
3. Add the grated cheddar.
4. Sprinkle on 1/2 of your herbs.
5. Roll up as tightly as possible. I find that using baking paper or cling film works well here.
6. Slice into 1 inch (2.5cm) slices.
7. Pop into the air fryer basket.
8. Bake at 200°C/400°F for 6-7 minutes until golden brown.

Air Fryer Mommy Hot Dogs

Servings: 4-6
Cooking Time: 9 Mints
Ingredients:

- 227 g refrigerated crescent dough or crescent dough sheets , see headnote
- 8 hot dogs
- mustard
- ketchup or hot sauce
- oil spray

Directions:

1. Unroll the crescent dough. Cut into 3/8"-1/2" (9mm-13mm) wide strips.
2. Pat the hot dogs dry (helps keep the dough from slipping around while rolling).Wrap a couple pieces of dough around each hot dog to look like bandages. Criss-cross them occasionally and make sure to leave a separation of the bandages on one end for the face. Stretch the dough if needed.
3. lightly spray the ends of the wrapped hot dogs with oil spray. Spray the air fryer basket with oil spray.Lay the wrapped hot dogs face-side up in the air fryer basket or tray, making sure the mummies aren't touching
4. Air Fry at 330°F (166°C) for 6 minutes. Gently wiggle to loosen from the baskets.Air Fry at 330°F (166°C) for another 1-3 minutes or until crescent dough is golden, and cooked through.

Polenta Fries

Servings: 6
Cooking Time: X
Ingredients:

- 800 ml/scant 3½ cups water
- 1½ vegetable stock cubes
- ¾ teaspoon dried oregano
- ¾ teaspoon freshly ground black pepper
- 200 g/1⅓ cups quick-cook polenta/cornmeal
- 2 teaspoons olive oil
- 55 g/6 tablespoons plain/all-purpose flour (gluten-free if you wish)
- garlic mayonnaise, to serve

Directions:

1. Bring the water and stock cubes to the boil in a saucepan with the oregano and black pepper. Stir in the polenta/cornmeal and continue to stir until the mixture becomes significantly more solid and is hard to stir – this should take about 5–6 minutes.
2. Grease a 15 x 15-cm/6 x 6-in. baking pan with some of the olive oil. Tip the polenta into the baking pan, smoothing down with the back of a wet spoon. Leave to cool at room temperature for about 30 minutes, then pop into the fridge for at least an hour.
3. Remove the polenta from the fridge and carefully tip out onto a chopping board. Slice the polenta into fingers 7.5 x 1 x 2 cm/3 x ½ x ¾ in. Roll the polenta fingers in the flour, then spray or drizzle the remaining olive oil over the fingers.
4. Preheat the air-fryer to 200ºC/400ºF.
5. Lay the fingers apart from one another in a single layer in the preheated air-fryer (you may need to cook these in batches, depending on the size of your air-fryer). Air-fry for 9 minutes, turning once halfway through cooking. Serve immediately with garlic mayonnaise.

Air Fryer Baked Egg Cups W Spinach & Cheese

Servings: 1
Cooking Time: 10 Mints
Ingredients:

- 1 large (1 large) egg
- 1 tablespoon milk or half & half
- 1 tablespoon frozen spinach , thawed (or sautéed fresh spinach)
- 1-2 teaspoons grated cheese
- salt , to taste
- black pepper, to taste
- Cooking Spray, for muffin cups or ramekins

Directions:

1. Spray inside of silicone muffin cups or ramekin with oil spray. Add egg, milk, spinach and cheese into the muffin cup or ramekin.
2. Add salt, pepper or seasonings to the egg. Gently stir ingredients into egg whites without breaking the yolk.
3. Air Fry at 330°F/165°C for about 6-12 minutes (single egg cups usually take about 6 minutes – multiple or doubled up cups take as much as 12. As you add more egg cups, you will need to add more time.)
4. Timing Note: Cooking in a ceramic ramekin may take a little longer. If you want runny yolks, cook for less time. Keep checking the eggs after 5 minutes to ensure the egg is to your preferred texture.

Avocado Fries

Servings: 2
Cooking Time: X
Ingredients:

- 35 g/¼ cup plain/all-purpose flour (gluten free if you wish)
- ½ teaspoon chilli/chili powder
- 1 egg, beaten
- 50 g/heaped ½ cup dried breadcrumbs
- 1 avocado, skin and stone removed, and each half sliced lengthways
- salt and freshly ground black pepper

Directions:

1. Preheat the air-fryer to 200°C/400°F.
2. In a bowl combine the flour and chilli/chili powder, then season with salt and pepper. Place the beaten egg in a second bowl and the breadcrumbs in a third bowl.
3. Dip each avocado slice in the seasoned flour (shaking off any excess), then the egg and finally the breadcrumbs.
4. Add the breaded avocado slices to the preheated air-fryer and air-fry for 6 minutes, turning after 4 minutes. Serve immediately.

Beetroot Crisps

Servings: 2

Ingredients:

- 3 medium beetroots
- 2 tbsp oil
- Salt to taste

Directions:

1. Peel and thinly slice the beetroot
2. Coat with the oil and season with salt
3. Preheat the air fryer to 200ºC
4. Place in the air fryer and cook for 12-18 minutes until crispy

Ultra Crispy Air Fryer Chickpeas

Servings: 2

Cooking Time: 15 Mints

Ingredients:

- 250 g can of chickpeas (drained and rinsed)
- 1 tablespoon olive oil
- ⅛ teaspoon salt
- ¼ teaspoon garlic powder
- ¼ teaspoon onion powder
- ½ teaspoon paprika

Directions:

1. Heat air fryer to 200°C/400° .
2. Drain and rinse chickpeas (no need to dry). Toss with olive oil and spices.
3. Dump the whole batch of chickpeas in the air fryer basket. Cook for 12-15 minutes, shaking a couple of times.
4. When chickpeas are cooked to your liking, remove from air fryer, taste and add more salt and pepper to taste.
5. Store in an open container.

Air Fryer Stuffed Zucchini Boats With Sausage

Servings: 4
Cooking Time: 10 Mints

Ingredients:

- 2 medium zucchini , halved and cored
- 227 g uncooked sausage meat
- 60 ml breadcrumbs
- 57 g grated cheese
- 2 Tablespoons fresh chopped parsley
- oil spray, for coating

Directions:

1. Halve and core the zucchini.
2. Lay zucchini cut-side down and spray skin side with olive oil spray.
3. Flip the zucchini and stuff the center with sausage. Top with breadcrumbs and cheese. Spray tops with oil spray.
4. Lay zucchini in air fryer making sure the zucchini doesn't tip over (see note below).
5. Air Fry at 360°F/180°C for 10-14 minutes or until sausage is cooked all the way through. Serve with sauce if you want. Top with parsley. It's delicious either way!

Air Fryer Cheeseburger

Servings: 4
Cooking Time: 10 Mints

Ingredients:

- 450 g beef mince
- 2 cloves garlic, crushed
- 1 tbsp. low-sodium soy sauce
- Salt
- Freshlyground black pepper
- 4 slices American cheese
- 4 hamburger buns
- Mayonnaise
- Lettuce
- Sliced tomatoes
- Thinly sliced red onion

Directions:

1. In a large bowl combine beef, garlic, and soy sauce. Shape into 4 patties and flatten into a 11cm circle. Season both sides with salt and pepper.
2. Place 2 patties in air fryer and cook at 180°C/350°F for 4 minutes per side, for medium. 3. Remove and immediately top with a slice of cheese. Repeat with the remaining 2 patties.
3. Spread hamburger buns with mayo, then top with lettuce, patties, tomatoes, and onions.

Cheese Scones

Servings: 12
Cooking Time: X

Ingredients:

- ½ teaspoon baking powder
- 210 g/1½ cups self-raising/self-rising flour (gluten-free if you wish), plus extra for dusting
- 50 g/3½ tablespoons cold butter, cubed
- 125 g/1½ cups grated mature Cheddar
- a pinch of cayenne pepper
- a pinch of salt
- 100 ml/7 tablespoons milk, plus extra for brushing the tops of the scones

Directions:

1. Mix the baking powder with the flour in a bowl, then add the butter and rub into the flour to form a crumblike texture. Add the cheese, cayenne pepper and salt and stir. Then add the milk, a little at a time, and bring together into a ball of dough.
2. Dust your work surface with flour. Roll the dough flat until about 1.5 cm/⅝ in. thick. Cut out the scones using a 6-cm/2½-in. diameter cookie cutter. Gather the offcuts into a ball, re-roll and cut more scones – you should get about 12 scones from the mixture. Place the scones on an air-fryer liner or a piece of pierced parchment paper.
3. Preheat the air-fryer to 180ºC/350ºF.
4. Add the scones to the preheated air-fryer and air-fry for 8 minutes, turning them over halfway to cook the other side. Remove and allow to cool a little, then serve warm.

Waffle Fries

Servings: 4

Ingredients:

- 2 large potatoes, russet potatoes work best
- 1 tsp salt for seasoning
- Waffle cutter

Directions:

1. Peel the potatoes and slice using the waffle cutter. You can also use a mandolin cutter that has a blade
2. Transfer the potatoes to a bowl and season with the salt, coating evenly
3. Add to the air fryer and cook at 220ºC for 15 minutes, shaking every so often

Air Fryer Mexican Street Corn-on-the-cob Elotes

Servings: 4
Cooking Time: 16 Mints

Ingredients:

- 4 ears (4 ears) corn , husked
- 2 Tablespoons (30 g) butter , melted (approximately)
- Kosher salt , to taste
- 60 mlmayonnaise
- 75 g finely crumbled cotija (or parmesan cheese or feta cheese) plus more for serving
- 1/2 teaspoon smoked paprika
- 1/2 teaspoon chili powder , plus more for serving
- 1 teaspoon garlic powder
- 60 ml finely chopped cilantro leaves , and extra for garnish (optional)
- 1/4 teaspoon kosher salt , or to taste
- fresh cracked black pepper , to taste
- 2 stalks green onions , sliced thin
- 1 lime , cut into wedges
- black pepper , to taste
- FOR CHEESE MIXTURE
- 80 ml Mexican cream or sour cream

Directions:

1. Cut the corn to the size of your air fryer basket or rack (some might need to be cut in half). Coat the corn with melted butter and season with salt and pepper.
2. Air Fry at 370°F (190°C) for about 12-16 minutes, turning the corn half way through cooking. Cook until kernels are tender and lightly browned. (Cooking time will depend on size of corn, how full the air fryer basket is, & different models/sizes of air fryers).
3. While the corn air frys, make the cheese mixture. In a bowl combine sour cream, mayonnaise, cheese, smoked paprika, chili powder, garlic powder, cilantro, salt and pepper in a large bowl. Mix until evenly combined.
4. After corn is cooked, spread the cheese mixture over the corn. Sprinkle with extra crumbled cheese, paprika or chili powder, green onions and/or chopped cilantro. Serve with lime wedges.

Air Fryer Frittata

Servings: 2
Cooking Time: 10 Mints

Ingredients:

- Oil or butter to grease the pan
- 3 eggs
- 1/4 red pepper, diced
- 1/4 green pepper, diced
- 10 baby spinach leaves, chopped
- Handful of cheddar cheese, grated
- Salt and pepper to season, optional

Dirctions:

1. In a bowl beat the eggs. Season with salt and pepper if required.
2. Grease the pan with the oil or butter and place it in the air fryer. Switch to 180°C/350°F and allow to heat for a minute. Add the peppers and cook for 3 minutes.
3. Pour the spinach and egg mix in. Sprinkle the grated cheese across the top. Cook for a further 6 minutes, checking half way through to make sure it isn't over cooking

Air Fryer Gozleme Danish

Servings: 2
Cooking Time: 20 Mints
Ingredients:

- 2 tsp rice bran oil
- ¼ medium brown onion, finely chopped
- 80 g frozen spinach, thawed, excess water squeezed out
- 1 sheet frozen puff pastry, just thawed
- 200 g Danish feta, halved horizontally
- 1 egg yolk, lightly whisked

Directions:

1. Heat the oil in a small frying pan over medium-high heat. Add onion and cook, stirring, for 4-5 minutes or until golden. Add the spinach and cook, stirring, for 30 seconds or until combined. Remove from heat. Set aside to cool.
2. Place the pastry on a large chopping board. Place the feta in the centre. Top with onion mixture. Slice pastry diagonally into 2cm-wide strips along the long sides of the filling. Fold in the short ends. Fold 1 strip of pastry over the filling, then fold in another strip from the opposite side, slightly overlapping. Continue alternating the strips over the filling until completely enclosed. Discard excess pastry or save for another use.
3. Place in an air fryer and brush with egg. Cook at 180°C/350°F for 15 minutes or until crisp and golden.Cut into slices. Serve with lemon wedges, if using

Potato Patties

Servings: 12
Ingredients:

- 150g instant mash
- 50g peas and carrots
- 2 tbsp coriander
- 1 tbsp oil
- 100ml hot water
- ½ tsp turmeric
- ½ tsp cayenne
- ½ tsp salt
- ½ tsp cumin seeds
- ¼ tsp ground cumin

Directions:

1. Place all the ingredients in a bowl. Mix well cover and stand for 10 minutes
2. Preheat the air fryer to 200ºC
3. Spray the air fryer with cooking spray
4. Make 12 patties, place in the air fryer and cook for 10 minutes

Sweet Potato Crisps

Servings: 4

Ingredients:

- 1 sweet potato, peeled and thinly sliced
- 2 tbsp oil
- ¼ tsp salt
- ¼ tsp pepper
- 1 tsp chopped rosemary
- Cooking spray

Directions:

1. Place all ingredients in a bowl and mix well
2. Place in the air fryer and cook at 175ºC for about 15 minutes until crispy

Air Fryer Pasta Chips

Servings: 4

Cooking Time: 10 Mints

Ingredients:

- 227 g dried Bowtie (Farfalle) Pasta, or pasta shape of choice
- 1 Tablespoon Olive Oil or Vegetable Oil
- 1 teaspoon Garlic Powder
- 35 g Parmesan Cheese
- 1/2 teaspoon Kosher Salt, or to taste

Directions:

1. In a large pot of salted boiling water, cook the pasta to package directions. Cook until it is tender.
2. Drain the pasta and put in a bowl. Toss with the olive oil, garlic powder, parmesan cheese, and cook in batches if needed.
3. Cooking in batches if needed, put just a single layer of the seasoned pasta in the air fryer basket/tray.
4. Air Fry at 380°F/195°C for 7-10 minutes, shaking and stirring the pasta every 2-3 minutes making sure to separate any pasta sticking together.
5. Cook until the pasta is golden and crispy to your liking.

Spicy Egg Rolls

Servings: 4

Ingredients:

- 1 rotisserie chicken, shredded and diced
- 3 tbsp water
- 3 tbsp taco seasoning
- 1 can of black beans, drained
- 1 red bell pepper, diced
- 1 can of sweetcorn, drained
- 1 jalapeño pepper, deseeded and minced
- 2 packs of egg roll wrappers
- 250g grated strong cheddar cheese
- 250g grated Monterey Jack cheese

Directions:

1. Take a medium bowl and add the water and taco seasoning, combining well
2. Add the shredded check and coat well
3. Lay out an egg roll wrapper and arrange it so that one corner is facing towards you
4. Add 3 tablespoons of the mixture into the wrapper, just below the middle
5. Roll the corner facing you upwards, pulling it tightly closed over the mixture
6. Add a little water to the other two corners and fold into the centre and pat down to seal
7. Roll the rest of the wrapper up, so that all the corners are sealed
8. Repeat with the rest of the mixture
9. Preheat the air fryer to 220ºC
10. Cook for 9 minutes and turn over at the halfway point

Spring Rolls

Servings: 20

Ingredients:

- 160g dried rice noodles
- 1 tsp sesame oil
- 300g minced beef
- 200g frozen vegetables
- 1 onion, diced
- 3 cloves garlic, crushed
- 1 tsp soy sauce
- 1 tbsp vegetable oil
- 1 pack egg roll wrappers

Directions:

1. Soak the noodles in a bowl of water until soft
2. Add the minced beef, onion, garlic and vegetables to a pan and cook for 6 minutes
3. Remove from the heat, stir in the noodles and add the soy
4. Heat the air fryer to 175ºC
5. Add a diagonal strip of filling in each egg roll wrapper
6. Fold the top corner over the filling, fold in the two side corners
7. Brush the centre with water and roll to seal
8. Brush with vegetable oil, place in the air fryer and cook for about 8 minutes until browned

Beef & Lamb And Pork Recipes

Air Fryer Frozen Meatballs

Servings: 3
Cooking Time: 10 Mints
Ingredients:

- 454 g Frozen Meatballs
- oil spray , to coat the meatballs
- BBQ or Tomato Sauce, optional

Directions:

1. Cook Frozen – Do not thaw first.
2. Shake or turn as needed. Don't overcrowd the air fryer basket.
3. Recipe timing is based on a non-preheated air fryer. If cooking in multiple batches back to back, the following batches may cook a little quicker.
4. Recipes were tested in 3.7 to 6 qt. air fryers. If you use a larger air fryer, they might cook quicker, so adjust cooking time.
5. Remember to set a timer to shake/flip/toss as directed in recipe.

Tender Ham Steaks

Servings: 1
Ingredients:

- 1 ham steak
- 2 tbsp brown sugar
- 1 tsp honey
- 2 tbsp melted butter

Directions:

1. Preheat the air fryer to 220°C
2. Combine the melted butter and brown sugar until smooth
3. Add the ham to the air fryer and brush both sides with the butter mixture
4. Cook for 12 minutes, turning halfway through and re-brushing the ham
5. Drizzle honey on top before serving

Beef Fried Rice

Servings: 2

Ingredients:

- 400g cooked rice
- 250g cooked beef strips
- 1 tbsp sesame oil
- 1 diced onion
- 1 egg
- 2 tsp garlic powder
- Salt and pepper
- 1 tbsp vegetable oil
- 250g frozen peas

Directions:

1. Preheat air fryer to 175°C
2. Season the beef with salt, pepper and garlic powder, cook in a pan until about ¾ cooked
3. Mix the rice with peas carrots and vegetable oil, add the beef and mix
4. Add to the air fryer and cook for about 10 minutes
5. Add the egg and cook until the egg is done

Beef Satay

Servings: 2

Ingredients:

- 400g steak strips
- 2 tbsp oil
- 1 tbsp fish sauce
- 1 tsp sriracha sauce
- 200g sliced coriander (fresh)
- 1 tsp ground coriander
- 1 tbsp soy
- 1 tbsp minced ginger
- 1 tbsp minced garlic
- 1 tbsp sugar
- 25g roasted peanuts

Directions:

1. Add oil, dish sauce, soy, ginger, garlic, sugar sriracha, coriander and ¼ cup coriander to a bowl and mix. Add the steak and marinate for 30 minutes
2. Add the steak to the air fryer and cook at 200°C for about 8 minutes
3. Place the steak on a plate and top with remaining coriander and chopped peanuts
4. Serve with peanut sauce

Pork Chilli Cheese Dogs

Servings: 2

Ingredients:

- 1 can of pork chilli, or chilli you have left over
- 200g grated cheese
- 2 hot dog bread rolls
- 2 hot dogs

Directions:

1. Preheat the air fryer to 260°C
2. Cook the hot dogs for 4 minutes, turning halfway
3. Place the hotdogs inside the bread rolls and place back inside the air fryer
4. Top with half the cheese on top and then the chilli
5. Add the rest of the cheese
6. Cook for an extra 2 minutes

Lamb Koftas

Servings: 3

Cooking Time: X

Ingredients:

- 600 g/1 lb. 5 oz. minced/ground lamb
- 1 onion, finely chopped
- 1 garlic clove, finely chopped
- 2 tablespoons finely chopped coriander/cilantro
- 1 teaspoon ground coriander
- 1 teaspoon ground cumin
- 1 teaspoon ground turmeric
- ½ teaspoon chilli/chili powder
- 1 teaspoon dried thyme
- 1 teaspoon salt
- 1 tablespoon runny honey

Directions:

1. Combine all the ingredients in a bowl and mix together well. Divide into 6 equal portions and mould into sausage shapes. Place in the fridge for at least an hour before cooking.
2. Preheat the air-fryer to 180°C/350°F.
3. Thread a small metal skewer through each kofta. Place in the preheated air-fryer and air-fry for 10 minutes, turning halfway through cooking. Check the internal temperature of the koftas has reached at least 70°C/160°F using a meat thermometer – if not, cook for another few minutes and then serve.

Herby Lamb Chops

Servings: 4
Cooking Time: X
Ingredients:

- 8 lamb chops
- 1 teaspoon dried oregano
- 1 tablespoon olive oil
- salt and freshly ground black pepper

Directions:

1. Drizzle the oil over both sides of the chops and season both sides with the oregano, salt and pepper (a good dose of both). Leave to marinate for 30 minutes at room temperature.
2. Preheat the air-fryer to 180ºC/350ºF.
3. Add the chops to the preheated air-fryer and air-fry for 5–7 minutes, turning once during cooking. Check the internal temperature of the chops has reached at least 55ºC/130ºF using a meat thermometer – if not, cook for another few minutes and then serve.

Beef Stroganoff

Servings:4
Cooking Time:20 Minutes
Ingredients:

- 4 cubes / 800 ml beef stock cubes
- 4 tbsp olive oil
- 1 onion, chopped
- 200 g / 7 oz sour cream
- 200 g / 7 oz mushroom, finely sliced
- 500 g / 17.6 oz steak, chopped
- 4 x 100 g / 3.5 oz egg noodles, cooked

Directions:

1. Preheat the air fryer to 200 °C / 400 °F and line the bottom of the basket with parchment paper.
2. Boil 800 ml of water and use it to dissolve the 4 beef stock cubes.
3. In a heat-proof bowl, mix the olive oil, onion, sour cream, mushrooms, and beef stock until fully combined.
4. Coat all sides of the steak chunks in the mixture and set aside to marinate for 10 minutes.
5. Transfer the steak to the air fryer, close the lid, and cook for 10 minutes. Serve the steak hot with a serving of egg noodles.

Tahini Beef Bites

Servings: 2

Ingredients:

- 500g sirloin steak, cut into cubes
- 2 tbsp Za'atar seasoning
- 1 tsp olive oil
- 25g Tahini
- 25g warm water
- 1 tbsp lemon juice
- 1 clove of garlic
- Salt to taste

Directions:

1. Preheat the air fryer to 250°C
2. Take a bowl and combine the oil with the steak, salt, and Za'atar seasoning
3. Place in the air fryer and cook for 10 minutes, turning halfway through
4. Take a bowl and combine the water, garlic, lemon juice, salt, and tahini, or use a food processor if you have one
5. Pour the sauce over the bites and serve

Mediterranean Beef Meatballs

Servings: 3

Cooking Time: X

Ingredients:

- 500 g/1 lb. 2 oz. minced/ground beef
- 30 g/½ cup fresh breadcrumbs (gluten-free if you wish)
- 1 egg
- 1 teaspoon dried thyme
- ¾ teaspoon salt
- ½ teaspoon freshly ground black pepper
- Mediterranean Sauce or 400-g/14-oz. jar tomato-based pasta sauce
- spaghetti, basil leaves and freshly grated Parmesan, to serve

Directions:

1. Combine all the ingredients (not the sauce) together in a bowl, then divide into 9 equal portions and mould into meatballs.
2. Preheat the air-fryer to 180°C/350°F.
3. Place the meatballs in the preheated air-fryer and air-fry for 8 minutes, turning halfway through cooking.
4. Pour the sauce into a baking dish or gratin dish that fits into your air-fryer. After 8 minutes, pop the meatballs into the sauce in the dish and put the whole dish back into the air-fryer. Cook for a further 5 minutes, then check the internal temperature of the meatballs has reached at least 70°C/160°F using a meat thermometer – if not, cook for another few minutes.
5. Serve the meatballs piled on top of spaghetti, garnished with basil leaves and scattered with grated Parmesan.

Pork Chops With Sprouts

Servings: 2

Ingredients:

- 300g pork chops
- ⅛ tsp salt
- ½ tsp pepper
- 250g Brussels sprouts quartered
- 1 tsp olive oil
- 1 tsp maple syrup
- 1 tsp dijon mustard

Directions:

1. Season the pork chops with salt and pepper
2. Mix together oil, maple syrup and mustard. Add Brussels sprouts
3. Add pork chops and Brussels sprouts to the air fryer and cook at 200°C for about 10 minutes

Southern Style Pork Chops

Servings: 4

Ingredients:

- 4 pork chops
- 3 tbsp buttermilk
- 100g flour
- Salt and pepper to taste
- Pork rub to taste

Directions:

1. Season the pork with pork rub
2. Drizzle with buttermilk
3. Coat in flour until fully covered
4. Place the pork chops in the air fryer, cook at 170°C for 15 minutes
5. Turnover and cook for a further 10 minutes

Air Fryer Rack Of Lamb

Servings: 2
Cooking Time: 15 Mints

Ingredients:

- 397 g/14 oz lamb rack
- 1 tbsp olive oil
- 1 tsp rosemary, fresh or dried
- 1 tsp thyme, fresh or dried
- ½ tsp salt
- ½ tsp black pepper

Directions:

1. Preheat air fryer to 360°F (180°C)
2. Mix olive oil with rosemary, thyme, salt and pepper on a large plate.
3. Pat lamb rack dry and press into the herb oil mixture, flip it over and rub the herb mix in so the lamb is well coated.
4. Place lamb rack in air fryer basket, and air fry for 15-20 minutes for medium done lamb.
5. Check the temperature with a meat thermometer to ensure that it is cooked to your liking (medium should be 130-135°F /54–57°C). Cook for additional 3 minute intervals if you prefer it more well done.
6. Remove lamb rack from air fryer, cover with kitchen foil and leave to rest for at least five minutes before serving.

Air Fryer Lamb Steaks

Servings: 2
Cooking Time: 7 Mints

Ingredients:

- 2 lamb steaks
- ½ teaspoon ground black pepper
- ½ teaspoon kosher salt
- Drizzle of light olive oil

Directions:

1. Remove steak from the refrigerator an hour before cooking to allow it to reach room temperature before cooking.
2. Preheat air fryer to 400°F/200°C.
3. Mix salt and ground pepper on a plate.
4. Pat lamb steaks dry, then rub or spray with a little olive oil.
5. Press each side of the steak into the salt/pepper mix, then place in air fryer basket. ensure they are not touching.
6. Air fry lamb steaks for 5 minutes for medium-rare (9 minutes for well-done).
7. Use an instant-read meat thermometer to check the internal temperature - it should be 160°F/71°C for medium-rare, or 170°F/76°C or above for well done. Remove lamb steaks from the air fryer, cover with foil and leave to rest for 5 minutes before serving.

Air Fryer "shake 'n Bake" Style Poek Chops

Servings: 10
Cooking Time: 30 Mints
Ingredients:

- 170 g pork chops , rinsed & patted dry
- Ice water, beaten egg, milk, or mayo , to moisten the pork

Directions:

1. Preheat Air Fryer at 380°F/195°C for 4 minutes.
2. Moisten the pork chops based on seasoned coating mix instructions (or by using ice water, beaten egg, milk, or mayo). Coat with the seasoned coating mix.
3. Spray an air fryer basket/tray with oil or place a perforated parchment sheet in the air fryer basket/tray & lightly coat with oil spray
4. Place the coated pork chops in a single layer (cook in batches if needed). Make sure pork chops are not touching or the coating may flake off when you flip them. Lightly coat the pork chops with oil spray.
5. Air Fry at 380°F/195°C for about 8-12 minutes. After 6 minutes of cooking, flip the pork chops and then continue cooking for the remainder of time or until golden and internal temperature reaches 145-160°F, depending on your doneness preference.

Lamb Calzone

Servings: 2
Ingredients:

- 1 tsp olive oil
- 1 chopped onion
- 100g baby spinach leaves
- 400g minced pork
- 250g whole wheat pizza dough
- 300g grated cheese

Directions:

1. Heat the olive oil in a pan, add the onion and cook for about 2 minutes
2. Add the spinach and cook for a further 1 ½ minutes
3. Stir in marinara sauce and the minced pork
4. Divide the dough into four and roll out into circles
5. Add ¼ of filling to each piece of dough
6. Sprinkle with cheese and fold the dough over to create half moons, crimp edges to seal
7. Spray with cooking spray, place in the air fryer and cook at 160ºC for 12 minutes turning after 8 minutes

Steak Dinner

Servings: 5

Ingredients:

- 400g sirloin steak, cut into cubes
- 300g red potatoes, cubed
- 1 pepper
- 1 tsp dried parsley
- ½ tsp pepper
- 2 tsp olive oil
- 1 sliced onion
- 300g chopped mushrooms
- 2 tsp garlic salt
- 2 tsp salt
- 5 tsp butter

Directions:

1. Preheat the air fryer to 200ºC
2. Take 5 pieces of foil, layer meat onion, potatoes, mushrooms and pepper in each one
3. Add 1 tsp of butter to each one
4. Mix seasonings and sprinkle over the top
5. Fold the foil and cook for 25-30 minutes

Salt And Pepper Belly Pork

Servings: 4

Ingredients:

- 500g belly pork
- 1 tsp pepper
- ½ tsp salt

Directions:

1. Cut the pork into bite size pieces and season with salt and pepper
2. Heat the air fryer to 200ºC
3. Place in the air fryer and cook for 15 minutes until crisp

Sausage Gnocchi One Pot

Servings: 2

Ingredients:

- 4 links of sausage
- 250g green beans, washed and cut into halves
- 1 tsp Italian seasoning
- 1 tbsp olive oil
- 300g gnocchi
- Salt and pepper for seasoning

Directions:

1. Preheat the air fryer to 220ºC
2. Cut the sausage up into pieces
3. Take a bowl and add the gnocchi and green beans, along with the oil and season
4. Place the sausage into the fryer first and then the rest of the ingredients
5. Cook for 12 minutes, giving everything a stir halfway through

Beef And Cheese Empanadas

Servings: 12

Ingredients:

- 2 tsp oil
- 1 chopped onion
- 1 clove chopped garlic
- 500g minced beef
- Salt and pepper
- 2 tbsp chopped jalapeño
- 2 packs ready made pastry
- 50g grated cheddar cheese
- 50g pepper jack cheese
- 1 egg

Directions:

1. Heat the oil in a pan and fry the onion and garlic until soft
2. Add the meat and jalapeño, season with salt and pepper, and cook until browned
3. Allow the meat to cool
4. Roll out dough as thin as possible and cut into circles, fill with 1 tablespoon of mix, sprinkle with cheese, fold over and seal with the egg
5. Set your fryer to 170ºC and cook for about 12 minutes until golden brown

All-day Breakfast

Servings: 1
Cooking Time: X

Ingredients:

- 1 medium tomato, sliced in half
- 1 large flat mushroom, thickly sliced
- 2 slices bacon
- 2 eggs (whole and in their shells)
- tomato ketchup, to serve
- hot buttered toast, to serve

Directions:

1. Preheat the air-fryer to 180°C/350°F.
2. Add the tomato halves to the preheated air-fryer and air-fry for 3 minutes. Add all other ingredients and cook for a further 6 minutes.
3. Serve everything together, with the eggs in egg cups. Add a generous dollop of tomato ketchup and hot buttered toast if you wish.

Poultry Recipes

Buffalo Chicken Wontons

Servings: 6

Ingredients:

- 200g shredded chicken
- 1 tbsp buffalo sauce
- 4 tbsp softened cream cheese
- 1 sliced spring onion
- 2 tbsp blue cheese crumbles
- 12 wonton wrappers

Directions:

1. Preheat the air fryer to 200°C
2. Take a bowl and combine the chicken and buffalo sauce
3. In another bowl mix the cream cheese until a smooth consistency has formed and then combine the scallion blue cheese and seasoned chicken
4. Take the wonton wrappers and run wet fingers along each edge
5. Place 1 tbsp of the filling into the centre of the wonton and fold the corners together
6. Cook at 200°C for 3 to 5 minutes, until golden brown

Quick Chicken Nuggets

Servings: 4

Ingredients:

- 500g chicken tenders
- 25g ranch salad dressing mixture
- 2 tbsp plain flour
- 100g breadcrumbs
- 1 egg, beaten
- Olive oil spray

Directions:

1. Take a large mixing bowl and arrange the chicken inside
2. Sprinkle the seasoning over the top and ensure the chicken is evenly coated
3. Place the chicken to one side for around 10 minutes
4. Add the flour into a resealable bag
5. Crack the egg into a small mixing bowl and whisk
6. Pour the breadcrumbs onto a medium sized plate
7. Transfer the chicken into the resealable bag and coat with the flour, giving it a good shake
8. Remove the chicken and dip into the egg, and then rolling it into the breadcrumbs, coating evenly
9. Repeat with all pieces of the chicken
10. Heat your air fryer to 200ºC
11. Arrange the chicken inside the fryer and add a little olive oil spray to avoid sticking
12. Cook for 4 minutes, before turning over and cooking for another 4 minutes
13. Remove and serve whilst hot

Satay Chicken Skewers

Servings: 4

Ingredients:

- 3 chicken breasts, chopped into 3 x 3-cm/1¼ x 1¼-in. cubes
- MARINADE
- 200 ml/¾ cup canned coconut milk (including the thick part from the can)
- 1 plump garlic clove, finely chopped
- 2 teaspoons freshly grated ginger
- 2 tablespoons soy sauce
- 1 heaped tablespoon peanut butter
- 1 tablespoon maple syrup
- 1 tablespoon mild curry powder
- 1 tablespoon fish sauce

Directions:

1. Mix the marinade ingredients thoroughly in a bowl, then toss in the chopped chicken and stir to coat thoroughly. Leave in the fridge to marinate for at least 4 hours.
2. Preheat the air-fryer to 190ºC/375ºF.
3. Thread the chicken onto 8 metal skewers. Add to the preheated air-fryer (you may need to cook these in two batches, depending on the size of your air-fryer). Air-fry for 10 minutes. Check the internal temperature of the chicken has reached at least 74ºC/165ºF using a meat thermometer – if not, cook for another few minutes and then serve.

Air Fryer Sesame Chicken Thighs

Servings: 4

Ingredients:

- 2 tbsp sesame oil
- 2 tbsp soy sauce
- 1 tbsp honey
- 1 tbsp sriracha sauce
- 1 tsp rice vinegar
- 400g chicken thighs
- 1 green onion, chopped
- 2 tbsp toasted sesame seeds

Directions:

1. Take a large bowl and combine the sesame oil, soy sauce, honey, sriracha and vinegar
2. Add the chicken and refrigerate for 30 minutes
3. Preheat the air fryer to 200ºC
4. Cook for 5 minutes
5. Flip and then cook for another 10 minutes
6. Serve with green onion and sesame seeds

Air Fryer Trader Joe's Frozen Kung Pao Chicken

Servings: 5

Cooking Time: 15 Mints

Ingredients:

- 652 g Trader Joe's Frozen Kung Pao Chicken
- optional – chopped cilantro &/or green onion , for garnish
- oil spray, for the veggie

Directions:

1. Place the frozen orange chicken in the air fryer basket and spread out into a single even layer. No oil spray is needed. Set the sauce, vegetables, and peanuts aside (do not sauce the chicken yet).
2. Air Fry at 380°F/195°C for 8 minutes. Add the vegetables (if you like the peanuts toastier you can add them now too) and shake/stir to combine with the chicken pieces. Spray with oil spray to lightly coat the vegetables.
3. While the chicken and vegetables air fry: Warm the sauce in microwave or on stovetop until heated through.
4. Continue to Air Fry at 380°F/195°C for another 3-6 minutes or until heated through.
5. Toss cooked chicken with as much sauce as you like, peanuts, optional cilantro and/or green onion and serve.

Jerk Chicken

Servings: 8
Cooking Time: 45 Mints

Ingredients:

- 8 chicken leg quarters or chicken drumsticks
- 80 ml apple cider vinegar
- 80 ml dark soy sauce
- 60 ml lime juice
- 120 ml orange juice
- 1 tbsp. allspice
- 1 tsp. black pepper

- 1 tsp. cinnamon
- 2 tsp. fresh thyme
- 3 spring onions, chopped
- 2 tbsp. ginger, peeled and chopped
- 1 medium onion, chopped
- 8 garlic cloves, peeled
- 4 Scotch bonnets, seeds removed

Directions:

1. Pat the skin of your chicken dry and using a knife make small holes all around the chicken.
2. In a blender combine all remaining ingredients and blend for three minutes. Pour half the jerk marinade over the chicken and massage it in. Refrigerate overnight.
3. When ready to cook, bring grill temperature up to 165°C/330°F. Place the chicken skin side down and close BBQ lid for 5-7 minutes until it starts to brown. Turn over and cook for the remaining 5-7 minutes. Repeat twice more until chicken is dark brown and cooked all the way through.
4. Move chicken to the sides of the grill and brush remaining jerk sauce on top. Close the lid and cook for a further 5-7minutes.
5. Remove from BBQ and leave chicken to cool for around 10 minutes. Either eat on the bone or chop the meat into smaller pieces and serve.

Hawaiian Chicken

Servings: 2

Ingredients:

- 2 chicken breasts
- 1 tbsp butter
- A pinch of salt and pepper
- 160ml pineapple juice
- 25g brown sugar

- 3 tbsp soy sauce
- 2 tsp water
- 1 clove of garlic, minced
- 1 tsp grated ginger
- 2 tsp cornstarch

Directions:

1. Preheat the air fryer to 260°C
2. Take a bowl and combine the butter and salt and pepper
3. Cover the chicken with the butter and cook in the fryer for 15 minutes, turning halfway
4. Remove and allow to rest for 5 minutes
5. Take another bowl and mix together the pineapple juice, soy sauce, garlic, ginger, and brown sugar
6. Transfer to a saucepan and simmer for 5 minutes
7. Combine the water and cornstarch and add to the sauce, stirring continually for another minute
8. Slice the chicken into strips and pour the sauce over the top

Air Fryer Spicy Chiken Thights

Servings: 4
Cooking Time: 10 Mints

Ingredients:

- 80 ml low-sodium soy sauce
- 60 ml extra-virgin olive oil
- 2 tbsp. honey
- 2 tbsp. chilli garlic sauce
- Juice of 1 lime
- 2 cloves garlic, crushed
- 2 tsp. freshly grated ginger
- 4 bone-in, skin-on chicken thighs
- Thinly sliced spring onions, for garnish
- Toasted sesame seeds, for garnish

Directions:

1. In a large bowl, combine soy sauce, oil, honey, chilli garlic sauce, lime juice, garlic, and ginger. Reserve 120ml of marinade. Add chicken thighs to bowl and toss to coat. Cover and refrigerate for at least 30 minutes.
2. Remove 2 thighs from marinade and place in basket of air fryer. Cook at 200°C/400°F until thighs are cooked through to an internal temperature of 73°C/165°F, 15 to 20 minutes. Transfer thighs to a plate and tent with foil. Repeat with remaining thighs.
3. Meanwhile, in a small saucepan over medium heat, bring reserved marinade to a boil. Reduce heat and simmer until sauce thickens slightly, 4 to 5 minutes.
4. Brush sauce over thighs and garnish with spring onions and sesame seeds before serving

Chicken Kiev

Servings: 4

Ingredients:

- 4 boneless chicken breasts
- 4 tablespoons plain/all-purpose flour (gluten-free if you wish)
- 1 egg, beaten
- 130 g/2 cups dried breadcrumbs (gluten-free if you wish, see page 9)
- GARLIC BUTTER
- 60 g/4 tablespoons salted butter, softened
- 1 large garlic clove, finely chopped

Directions:

1. Mash together the butter and garlic. Form into a sausage shape, then slice into 4 equal discs. Place in the freezer until frozen.
2. Make a deep horizontal slit across each chicken breast, taking care not to cut through to the other side. Stuff the cavity with a disc of frozen garlic butter. Place the flour in a shallow bowl, the egg in another and the breadcrumbs in a third Coat each chicken breast first in flour, then egg, then breadcrumbs.
3. Preheat the air-fryer to 180°C/350°F.
4. Add the chicken Kievs to the preheated air-fryer and air-fry for 12 minutes until cooked through. This is hard to gauge as the butter inside the breast is not an indicator of doneness, so test the meat in the centre with a meat thermometer – it should be at least 75°C/167°F; if not, cook for another few minutes.

Turkey And Mushroom Burgers

Servings: 2

Ingredients:

- 180g mushrooms
- 500g minced turkey
- 1 tbsp of your favourite chicken seasoning, e.g. Maggi
- 1 tsp onion powder
- 1 tsp garlic powder
- Salt and pepper to taste

Directions:

1. Place the mushrooms in a food processor and puree
2. Add all the seasonings and mix well
3. Remove from the food processor and transfer to a mixing bowl
4. Add the minced turkey and combine again
5. Shape the mix into 5 burger patties
6. Spray with cooking spray and place in the air fryer
7. Cook at 160ºC for 10 minutes, until cooked.

Air Fryer Hunters Chicken

Servings: 4-6

Cooking Time: 20 Mints

Ingredients:

- Spray oil
- 2 Chicken breasts
- 4 pieces of smoked streaky bacon
- 40 g grated cheddar or mozzarella / cheddar mix
- 50 ml BBQ sauce

Directions:

1. Season your chicken breasts well.
2. Lightly spray the chicken breasts with a little oil.
3. Cook at 200°C/400°F for 10 minutes.
4. Wrap each chicken breast with two pieces of streaky bacon.
5. Cook at 200°C/400°F for 6 minutes.
6. Spread on the BBQ sauce and add the grated cheddar carefully.
7. Cook at 200°C/400°F for another 4-5 minutes.
8. Check the temperature of your air fryer hunters chicken before serving, to ensure it is a minimum of 74°C/165°F internally.

Air Fryer Chicken Thighs

Servings: 4
Cooking Time: 12 Mints
Ingredients:

- 454 g skinless chicken thighs
- 3 tablespoons chicken spices
- 2 tablespoons light olive oil

Directions:

1. Preheat air fryer to 400°F/200°C.
2. Pat chicken thighs dry. Drizzle with oil and sprinkle with chicken spices, turn to ensure they are evenly coated with the oil and spice.
3. Place chicken thighs in an air fryer basket in a single layer. Make sure they are not overlapping.
4. Place basket into air fryer and air fry chicken thighs for 12-15 minutes [Note 1], until they are cooked through, and have reached 165°F/ 74°C in the center of the thickest part [Note 2]. Cook for additional 2-3 minute intervals if required until they are done.
5. Remove from the air fryer to a plate, cover with aluminum foil and allow to rest for 5 minutes. This allows the juices to reabsorb ensuring you have juicy tender chicken thighs.

Air Fried Maple Chicken Thighs

Servings: 4
Ingredients:

- 200ml buttermilk
- ½ tbsp maple syrup
- 1 egg
- 1 tsp granulated garlic salt
- 4 chicken thighs with the bone in
- 140g all purpose flour
- 65g tapioca flour
- 1 tsp sweet paprika
- 1 tsp onion powder
- ¼ tsp ground black pepper
- ¼ tsp cayenne pepper
- ½ tsp granulated garlic
- ½ tsp honey powder

Directions:

1. Take a bowl and combine the buttermilk, maple syrup, egg and garlic powder
2. Transfer to a bag and add chicken thighs, shaking to combine well
3. Set aside for 1 hour
4. Take a shallow bowl and add the flour, tapioca flour, salt, sweet paprika, smoked paprika, pepper, cayenne pepper and honey powder, combining well
5. Preheat the air fryer to 190ºC
6. Drag the chicken through flour mixture and place the chicken skin side down in the air fryer Cook for 12 minutes, until white in the middle

Air Fryer Chicken Tenders

Servings: 4
Cooking Time: 15 Mints
Ingredients:

- 675 g chicken tenders
- Salt
- Freshly ground black pepper
- 195 g plain flour
- 250 g panko bread crumbs
- 2 large eggs
- 60 ml buttermilk
- Cooking spray

- FOR THE HONEY MUSTARD
- 3 tbsp. honey
- 2 tbsp. dijon mustard
- 1/4 tsp. hot sauce (optional)
- Pinch of salt
- 80 g mayonnaise
- Freshlyground black pepper

Directions:

1. Season chicken tenders on both sides with salt and pepper. Place flour and bread crumbs in two separate shallow bowls. In a third bowl, whisk together eggs and buttermilk. Working one at a time, dip chicken in flour, then egg mixture, and finally in bread crumbs, pressing to coat.
2. Working in batches, place chicken tenders in basket of air fryer, being sure to not overcrowd it. Spray the tops of chicken with cooking spray and cook at 200°C/400°F for 5 minutes. Flip chicken over, spray the tops with more cooking spray and cook 5 minutes more. Repeat with remaining chicken tenders.
3. Make sauce: In a small bowl, whisk together mayonnaise, honey, dijon, and hot sauce, if using. Season with a pinch of salt and a few cracks of black pepper.
4. Serve chicken tenders with honey mustard

Air Fryer Chicken Breast

Servings: 2
Cooking Time: 10 Mints
Ingredients:

- 1 large egg, beaten
- 30 g plain flour
- 75 g panko bread crumbs
- 35 g freshly grated Parmesan
- 2 tsp. lemon zest

- 1 tsp.dried oregano
- 1/2 tsp. cayenne pepper
- Salt
- Freshlyground black pepper
- 2 boneless skinless chicken breasts

Directions:

1. Place eggs and flour in two separate shallow bowls. In a third shallow bowl, combine panko, Parmesan, lemon zest, oregano, and cayenne. Season with salt and pepper.
2. Working one at a time, dip chicken into flour, then eggs, and then panko mixture, pressing to coat.
3. Place in air fryer basket and cook at 190°C/375°F for 10 minutes. Flip chicken, and cook for another 5 minutes, until coating is golden and chicken is cooked through

Air Fryer Chicken Parmesan

Servings: 4
Cooking Time: 10 Mints

Ingredients:

- 2 large boneless chicken breasts
- Salt
- Freshlyground black pepper
- 40 g plain flour
- 2 large eggs
- 100 g panko bread crumbs
- 25 g freshly grated Parmesan

- 1 tsp. dried oregano
- 1/2 tsp.
- garlic powder
- 1/2 tsp. chilli flakes
- 240 g marinara/tomato sauce
- 100 g grated mozzarella
- Freshly chopped parsley, for garnish

Directions:

1. Pat the skin of your chicken dry and using a knife make small holes all around the chicken.
2. In a blender combine all remaining ingredients and blend for three minutes. Pour half the jerk marinade over the chicken and massage it in. Refrigerate overnight.
3. When ready to cook, bring grill temperature up to 165°C/330°F. Place the chicken skin side down and close BBQ lid for 5-7 minutes until it starts to brown. Turn over and cook for the remaining 5-7 minutes. Repeat twice more until chicken is dark brown and cooked all the way through.
4. Move chicken to the sides of the grill and brush remaining jerk sauce on top. Close the lid and cook for a further 5-7minutes.
5. Remove from BBQ and leave chicken to cool for around 10 minutes. Either eat on the bone or chop the meat into smaller pieces and serve.

Orange Chicken

Servings: 2

Ingredients:

- 600g chicken thighs, boneless and skinless
- 2 tbsp cornstarch
- 60ml orange juice
- 1 tbsp soy sauce
- 2 tbsp brown sugar

- 1 tbsp rice wine vinegar
- 1/4 teaspoon ground ginger
- Pinch of red pepper flakes
- Zest of one orange
- 2 tsp water and 2 tsp cornstarch mixed together

Directions:

1. Preheat your air fryer to 250°C
2. Take a bowl and combine the chicken with the cornstarch
3. Place in the air fryer and cook for 9 minutes
4. Take a bowl and combine the rest of the ingredients, except for the water and cornstarch mixture
5. Place in a saucepan and bring to the boil and then turn down to a simmer for 5 minutes
6. Add the water and cornstarch mixture to the pan and combine well
7. Remove the chicken from the fryer and pour the sauce over the top

Healthy Bang Bang Chicken

Servings: 4

Ingredients:

- 500g chicken breasts, cut into pieces of around 1" in size
- 1 beaten egg
- 50ml milk
- 1 tbsp hot pepper sauce
- 80g flour
- 70g tapioca starch
- 1 ½ tsp seasoned starch
- 1 tsp garlic granules
- ½ tsp cumin
- 6 tbsp plain Greek yogurt
- 3 tbsp sweet chilli sauce
- 1 tsp hot sauce

Directions:

1. Preheat the air fryer to 190ºC
2. Take a mixing bowl and combine the egg, milk and hot sauce
3. Take another bowl and combine the flour, tapioca starch, salt, garlic and cumin
4. Dip the chicken pieces into the sauce bowl and then into the flour bowl
5. Place the chicken into the air fryer
6. Whilst cooking, mix together the Greek yogurt, sweet chilli sauce and hot sauce and serve with the chicken

Whole Chicken

Servings: 4

Ingredients:

- 1.5-kg/3¼-lb. chicken
- 2 tablespoons butter or coconut oil
- salt and freshly ground black pepper

Directions:

1. Place the chicken breast-side up and carefully insert the butter or oil between the skin and the flesh of each breast. Season.
2. Preheat the air-fryer to 180ºC/350ºF. If the chicken hits the heating element, remove the drawer to lower the chicken a level.
3. Add the chicken to the preheated air-fryer breast-side up. Air-fry for 30 minutes, then turn over and cook for a further 10 minutes. Check the internal temperature with a meat thermometer. If it is 75ºC/167ºF at the thickest part, remove the chicken from the air-fryer and leave to rest for 10 minutes before carving. If less than 75ºC/167ºF, continue to cook until this internal temperature is reached and then allow to rest.

Nashville Chicken

Servings: 4

Ingredients:

- 400g boneless chicken breast tenders
- 2 tsp salt
- 2 tsp coarsely ground black pepper
- 2 tbsp hot sauce
- 2 tbsp pickle juice
- 500g all purpose flour
- 3 large eggs
- 300ml buttermilk
- 2 tbsp olive oil
- 6 tbsp cayenne pepper
- 3 tbsp dark brown sugar
- 1 tsp chilli powder
- 1 tsp garlic powder
- 1 tsp paprika
- Salt and pepper to taste

Directions:

1. Take a large mixing bowl and add the chicken, hot sauce, pickle juice, salt and pepper and combine
2. Place in the refrigerator for 3 hours
3. Transfer the flour to a bowl
4. Take another bowl and add the eggs, buttermilk and 1 tbsp of the hot sauce, combining well
5. Press each piece of chicken into the flour and coat well
6. Place the chicken into the buttermilk mixture and then back into the flour
7. Allow to sit or 10 minutes
8. Preheat the air fryer to 193C
9. Whisk together the spices, brown sugar and olive oil to make the sauce and pour over the chicken tenders
10. Serve whilst still warm

Chicken Fried Rice

Servings: 4

Ingredients:

- 400g cooked white rice
- 400g cooked chicken, diced
- 200g frozen peas and carrots
- 6 tbsp soy sauce
- 1 tbsp vegetable oil
- 1 diced onion

Directions:

1. Take a large bowl and add the rice, vegetable oil and soy sauce and combine well
2. Add the frozen peas, carrots, diced onion and the chicken and mix together well
3. Pour the mixture into a nonstick pan
4. Place the pan into the air fryer
5. Cook at 182C for 20 minutes

Fish & Seafood Recipes

Thai-style Tuna Fishcakes

Servings: 2

Ingredients:

- 2
- 00 g/7 oz. cooked potato
- 145 g/5 oz. canned tuna, drained
- 60 g/1 cup canned sweetcorn/corn kernels (drained weight)
- ½ teaspoon soy sauce
- ½ teaspoon fish sauce
- ½ teaspoon Thai 7 spice
- freshly squeezed juice of ½ a lime
- 1 teaspoon freshly grated garlic
- 1 teaspoon freshly grated ginger
- avocado or olive oil, for brushing
- LIME-ALMOND SATAY SAUCE
- 20 ml/4 teaspoons fresh lime juice
- 2 heaped tablespoons almond butter
- 1 teaspoon soy sauce
- ½ teaspoon freshly grated ginger
- ½ teaspoon freshly grated garlic
- ½ teaspoon avocado or olive oil
- ½ teaspoon maple syrup

Directions:

1. Combine all the fishcake ingredients in a food processor and blend together. Divide the mixture into 6 equal portions and mould into fishcakes. Brush a little oil over the top surface of the fishcakes.
2. Preheat the air-fryer to 180ºC/350ºF.
3. Place the fishcakes on an air-fryer liner or a piece of pierced parchment paper and add to the preheated air-fryer. Air-fry for 4 minutes, then turn over and brush the other side of each fishcake with oil and air-fry for a further 4 minutes.
4. To make the satay dipping sauce, mix all ingredients in a bowl with 1 tablespoon warm water. Serve alongside the fishcakes.

Traditional Fish And Chips

Servings: 4

Ingredients:

- 4 potatoes, peeled and cut into chips
- 2 fish fillets of your choice
- 1 beaten egg
- 1 lemon rind and juice
- 1 tbsp parsley
- Salt and pepper to taste
- 3 slices of wholemeal bread, grated into breadcrumbs
- 25g tortilla crisps

Directions:

1. Preheat your air fryer to 200ºC
2. Place the chips inside and cook until crispy
3. Cut the fish fillets into 4 slices and season with lemon juice
4. Place the breadcrumbs, lemon rind, parsley, tortillas and seasoning into a food processor and blitz to create a crumb consistency
5. Place the breadcrumbs on a large plate
6. Coat the fish in the egg and then the breadcrumb mixture
7. Cook for 15 minutes at 180ºC

Gluten Free Honey And Garlic Shrimp

Servings: 2

Ingredients:

- 500g fresh shrimp
- 5 tbsp honey
- 2 tbsp gluten free soy sauce
- 2 tbsp tomato ketchup
- 250g frozen stir fry vegetables
- 1 crushed garlic clove
- 1 tsp fresh ginger
- 2 tbsp cornstarch

Directions:

1. Simmer the honey, soy sauce, garlic, tomato ketchup and ginger in a saucepan
2. Add the cornstarch and whisk until sauce thickens
3. Coat the shrimp with the sauce
4. Line the air fryer with foil and add the shrimp and vegetables
5. Cook at 180ºC for 10 minutes

Beer Battered Fish Tacos

Servings: 2

Ingredients:

- 300g cod fillets
- 2 eggs
- 1 can of Mexican beer
- 300g cornstarch
- 300g flour
- 2 soft corn tortillas
- ½ tsp chilli powder
- 1 tbsp cumin
- Salt and pepper to taste

Directions:

1. Whisk together the eggs and beer
2. In a separate bowl whisk together cornstarch, chilli powder, flour, cumin and salt and pepper
3. Coat the fish in the egg mixture then coat in flour mixture
4. Spray the air fryer with non stick spray and add the fish
5. Set your fryer to 170ºC and cook for 15 minutes
6. Place the fish in a corn tortilla

Air Fried Shrimp Sub

Servings: 4
Cooking Time: 10 Mints
Ingredients:

- French rolls
- Remolade Sauce (found in the dressing aisle at any grocery store)
- Shredded lettuce
- Sliced tomatoes
- Gorton's Popcorn Shrimp

Directions:

1. Set your air fryer to 200°C/400° and toss in half the bag of your frozen popcorn shrimp. Cook for about 8 – 10 minutes, until reaching an internal temperature of 165°C/320°F or higher.
2. In the meantime, lather remoulade sauce on your French roll.
3. Once the shrimp is crispy, build your po' boy with lettuce and tomatoes. Enjoy!

Air Fryer Lobster Tails With Lemon-garlic Butter

Servings: 2
Cooking Time: 10 Mints
Ingredients:

- 2 lobster tails
- 4 tablespoons butter
- 1 teaspoon lemon zest
- 1 clove garlic, grated
- salt and ground black pepper to taste
- 1 teaspoon chopped fresh parsley
- 2 wedges lemon

Directions:

1. Preheat an air fryer to 380°F/195°C
2. Butterfly lobster tails by cutting lengthwise through the centers of the hard top shells and meat with kitchen shears. Cut to, but not through, the bottoms of the shells. Spread tail halves apart. Place tails in the air fryer basket with lobster meat facing up.
3. Melt butter in a small saucepan over medium heat. Add lemon zest and garlic; heat until garlic is fragrant, about 30 seconds.
4. Transfer 2 tablespoons of butter mixture to a small bowl and brush onto lobster tails; discard any remaining brushed butter to avoid contamination from uncooked lobster. Season lobster with salt and pepper.
5. Cook in the preheated air fryer until lobster meat is opaque, 5 to 7 minutes.
6. Spoon reserved butter from the saucepan over lobster meat. Top with parsley and serve with lemon wedges.

Air Fried Shrimp Po Boy

Servings: 6
Cooking Time: 5 Mints
Ingredients:

- 1 box of Popcorn Shrim
- 6 French Rolls or Brioche Hot Dog buns
- 57 g/4 tbsp unsalted butter
- 150 g/2 cups shredded lettuce
- 2 large tomatoes, sliced
- For the remoulade sauce:
- 230 g/1 cup mayonnaise
- 2 tbsp dijon mustard
- 1 tsp smoked paprika
- 1 tsp old bay seasoning
- 1 tsp horseradish
- 2 tbsp dill pickle relish
- 2 cloves garlic, minced
- 1 tsp hot sauce
- 2 green onions, finely chopped
- 2 tbsp lemon juice
- 1 tsp Worcestershire sauce
- 1/4 tsp sea salt
- 1/4 tsp ground black pepper

Directions:

1. Combine all ingredients for remoulade sauce and set on the side.
2. Cook half of the bag of the Popcorn Shrimp in your air fryer at 200°C/400°F for 8 – 10 minutes, until reaching an internal temperature of 165°C/320°F or higher.
3. Spread butter on french rolls and toast for 2-3 minutes.
4. Fill french rolls with lettuce, tomatoes, Popcorn Shrimp, and drizzled remoulade sauce. Serve and enjoy!

Mushrooms Stuffed With Crab

Servings: 2
Ingredients:

- 500g large mushrooms
- 2 tsp salt
- Half a diced red onion
- 2 diced celery sticks
- 300g lump crab
- 35g seasoned breadcrumbs
- 1 egg
- 1 tsp oregano
- 1 tsp hot sauce
- 50g grated Parmesan cheese

Directions:

1. Preheat to 260ºC
2. Take a baking sheet and arrange the mushrooms top down
3. Spray with a little cooking oil
4. Take a bowl and combine the onions, celery, breadcrumbs, egg, crab and half the cheese, oregano and hot sauce
5. Fill each mushroom with the mixture and make sure it's heaped over the top
6. Cover with the rest of the cheese
7. Place in the air fryer for 18 minutes

Peppery Lemon Shrimp

Servings: 2

Ingredients:

- 300g uncooked shrimp
- 1 tbsp olive oil
- 1 the juice of 1 lemon
- 0.25 tsp garlic powder
- 1 sliced lemon
- 1 tsp pepper
- 0.25 tsp paprika

Directions:

1. Heat the fryer to 200ºC
2. Take a medium sized mixing bowl and combine the lemon juice, pepper, garlic powder, paprika and the olive oil together
3. Add the shrimp to the bowl and make sure they're well coated
4. Arrange the shrimp into the basket of the fryer
5. Cook for between 6-8 minutes, until firm and pink

Crispy Cajun Fish Fingers

Servings: 2

Ingredients:

- 350 g/12 oz. cod loins
- 1 teaspoon smoked paprika
- ½ teaspoon cayenne pepper
- ½ teaspoon onion granules
- ¾ teaspoon dried oregano
- ¼ teaspoon dried thyme
- ½ teaspoon salt
- ½ teaspoon unrefined sugar
- 40 g/½ cup dried breadcrumbs (gluten-free if you wish, see page 9)
- 2 tablespoons plain/all-purpose flour (gluten-free if you wish)
- 1 egg, beaten

Directions:

1. Slice the cod into 6 equal fish 'fingers'. Mix the spices, herbs, salt and sugar together, then combine with the breadcrumbs. Lay out three bowls: one with flour, one with beaten egg and one with the Cajun-spiced breadcrumbs. Dip each fish finger into the flour, then the egg, then the breadcrumbs until fully coated.
2. Preheat the air-fryer to 180ºC/350ºF.
3. Add the fish to the preheated air-fryer and air-fry for 6 minutes, until cooked inside. Check the internal temperature of the fish has reached at least 75ºC/167ºF using a meat thermometer – if not, cook for another few minutes.

Alba Salad With Air Fried Butterfly Shrimp

Servings: 2
Cooking Time: 6 Mints
Ingredients:

- 250 g Butterfly Shrimp
- 5 cups arugula
- 12 g/½ cup Kalamata olives, pitted
- 56 g/2 oz Roquefort, crumbled
- 1 pear
- 1 avocado
- 1 tbsp freshly squeezed lemon juice or apple cider vinegar
- 1 tsp Dijon mustard
- ½ tsp kosher sea salt
- ¼ tsp freshly-cracked black pepper
- 2 celery stalks
- 112 g/4 oz canned mushrooms, drained
- For the dressing:
- 3 tbsp olive oil
- 1 small garlic clove

Directions:

1. Place Gorton's Butterfly Shrimp on air fryer rack and air fry at 200°C/400°F for 11 – 13 minutes, until reaching an internal temperature of 145°C/300°For higher.
2. Chop pear, avocado, and celery stalk into bite-sized pieces.
3. Add arugula, Calamata olives, crumbled Roquefort, drained mushrooms, chopped pear, and avocado to a medium bowl.
4. For the dressing, finely chop garlic clove. Add all ingredients in a small bowl and mix with a fork or whisk.
5. Gently mix in the Alba Salad Dressing. Add the salad to a medium serving platter. Top with the air fried Butterfly Shrimp. Enjoy!

Parmesan-coated Fish Fingers

Servings: 2
Ingredients:

- 350 g/12 oz. cod loins
- 1 tablespoon grated Parmesan
- 40 g/½ cup dried breadcrumbs (gluten-free if you wish, see page 9)
- 1 egg, beaten
- 2 tablespoons plain/all-purpose flour (gluten free if you wish)

Directions:

1. Slice the cod into 6 equal fish fingers/sticks.
2. Mix the Parmesan together with the breadcrumbs. Lay out three bowls: one with flour, one with beaten egg and the other with the Parmesan breadcrumbs. Dip each fish finger/stick first into the flour, then the egg and then the breadcrumbs until fully coated.
3. Preheat the air-fryer to 180ºC/350ºF.
4. Add the fish to the preheated air-fryer and air-fry for 6 minutes. Check the internal temperature of the fish has reached at least 75ºC/167ºF using a meat thermometer – if not, cook for another few minutes. Serve immediately.

Ranch Style Fish Fillets

Servings: 4

Ingredients:

- 200g bread crumbs
- 30g ranch-style dressing mix
- 2 tbsp oil
- 2 beaten eggs
- 4 fish fillets of your choice
- Lemon wedges to garnish

Directions:

1. Preheat air fryer to 180ºC
2. Mix the bread crumbs and ranch dressing mix together, add in the oil until the mix becomes crumbly
3. Dip the fish into the, then cover in the breadcrumb mix
4. Place in the air fryer and cook for 12-13 minutes

Crispy Nacho Prawns

Servings: 6

Ingredients:

- 1 egg
- 18 large prawns
- 1 bag of nacho cheese flavoured corn chips, crushed

Directions:

1. Wash the prawns and pat dry
2. Place the chips into a bowl
3. In another bowl, whisk the egg
4. Dip the prawns into the egg and then the nachos
5. Preheat the air fryer to 180ºC
6. Cook for 8 minutes

Air Fryer Tuna Mornay Parcels

Servings: 2-3
Cooking Time: 30 Mints

Ingredients:

- 30 g butter
- 2 green shallots, thickly sliced
- 2 tbsp plain flour
- 310ml /1 1/4 cups milk
- 80 g/1 cup coarsely grated cheddar
- 185 g can tuna in oil, drained, flaked
- 120 g /3/4 cup frozen mixed vegetables (peas and corn)
- 2 sheets frozen puff pastry, just thawed
- 1 egg, lightly whisked

Directions:

1. Heat the butter in a medium saucepan over medium heat until melted. Add the shallot and cook, stirring, for 2 minutes or until soft. Add the flour and cook, stirring, for 1 minute. Gradually add the milk, stirring constantly, until smooth. Bring to a simmer. Cook, stirring, for 2 minutes or until thickened slightly. Remove from heat and stir in the cheese . Transfer to a large bowl. Set aside to cool until room temperature.
2. Add the tuna and frozen veg to the white sauce and stir until just combined. Cut each pastry sheet into 4 squares. Place 1/4 cupful tuna mixture into the centre of each square. Fold corners of pastry towards the centre to enclose the filling. Pinch to seal.
3. Preheat air fryer to 190°C/320°F for 2 minutes. Brush parcels with egg. Grease the base of air fryer basket with oil. Place 4 parcels into the basket and cook for 8 minutes or until light golden. Turn and cook for a further 3 minutes or until golden. Repeat with remaining parcels. Serve.

Cajun Shrimp Boil

Servings: 6

Ingredients:

- 300g cooked shrimp
- 14 slices of smoked sausage
- 5 par boiled potatoes, cut into halves
- 4 mini corn on the cobs, quartered
- 1 diced onion
- 3 tbsp old bay seasoning
- Olive oil spray

Directions:

1. Combine all the ingredients in a bowl and mix well
2. Line the air fryer with foil
3. Place half the mix into the air fryer and cook at 200ºC for about 6 minutes, mix the ingredients and cook for a further 6 minutes.
4. Repeat for the second batch

Air Fryer Fish Fillets

Servings: 3
Cooking Time: 15 Mints
Ingredients:

- 1 pound (454 g) white fish fillets (cod, halibut, tilapia, etc.)
- 1 teaspoon (5 ml) kosher salt , or to taste
- 1/2 teaspoon (2.5 ml) black pepper , or to taste
- 1 teaspoon (5 ml) garlic powder
- 1 teaspoon (5 ml) paprika
- 1-2 cups (60-120 g) breading of choice breadcrumbs, panko, crushed pork rinds or almond flour
- 1 egg , or more if needed

Directions:

1. Preheat the Air Fryer at 380°F/193°C for 4 minutes.
2. Cut fish filets in half if needed. Make sure they are even sized so they'll cook evenly.
3. Pat the filets dry. Lightly oil the filets and then season with salt, black pepper, garlic powder, and paprika.
4. Put the breading in a shallow bowl. In another bowl, beat the eggs. Dip the filets in the egg, shaking off excess egg. Dredge the filets in your breading of choice. Press filets into the bowl of breading so that they completely coat the filets. Repeat this process for all fish pieces.
5. Lightly spray parchment paper with oil spray. Lay coated fish in a single layer on parchment (cook in batches if needed). Generously spray all sides of the breaded filets with oil spray to coat any dry spots.
6. Air Fry at 380°F/193°C for 8-14 minutes, depending on the size and thickness of your filets. After 6 minutes, flip the filets. Lightly spray any dry spots than then continue cooking for the remaining time or until they are crispy brown and the fish is cooked through. Serve with your favorite dip: tartar sauce, mustard, aioli, etc

Lobster Tails

Servings: 2
Ingredients:

- 4 lobster tails
- 2 tbsp melted butter
- ½ tsp salt
- 1 tsp pepper

Directions:

1. Cut the lobster tails through the tail section and pull back the shell
2. Brush with the melted butter and sprinkle with salt and pepper
3. Heat the air fryer to 200ºC and cook for 4 minutes
4. Brush with melted butter and cook for a further 2 minutes

Honey Sriracha Salmon

Servings: 2

Ingredients:

- 25g sriracha
- 25g honey
- 500g salmon fillets
- 1 tbsp soy sauce

Directions:

1. Mix the honey, soy sauce and sriracha, keep half the mix to one side for dipping
2. Place the salmon in the sauce skin side up and marinade for 30 minutes
3. Spray air fryer basket with cooking spray
4. Heat the air fryer to 200ºC
5. Place salmon in the air fryer skin side down and cook for 12 minutes

Air Fryer Crab Cakes

Servings: 6

Cooking Time: 5 Mins

Ingredients:

- 60 g mayonnaise
- 1 egg
- 2 tbsp. chives, finely chopped
- 2 tsp. Dijon mustard
- 2 tsp. cajun seasoning
- 1 tsp. lemon zest
- 1/2 tsp. salt
- 450 g jumbo lump crab meat
- 120 g Cracker crumbs (from about 20 crackers)
- Cooking spray
- Hot sauce, for serving
- Lemon wedges, for serving
- FOR THE TARTAR SAUCE
- 60 g mayonnaise
- 80 1/2 g dill pickle, finely chopped
- 1 tbsp. shallot, finely chopped
- 2 tsp. capers, finely chopped
- 1 tsp. fresh lemon juice
- 1/4 tsp. Dijon mustard
- 1 tsp. fresh dill, finely chopped

Directions:

1. Make crab cakes: In a large bowl, whisk together mayo, egg, chives, Dijon mustard, cajun seasoning, lemon zest and salt. Fold in the crab meat and the cracker crumbs.
2. Divide the mixture equally, forming 8 patties. You can refrigerate them for up to 4 hours if you're not ready to fry them. (Patties can also be frozen on a parchment-lined baking tray.)
3. Heat the air fryer to 190ºC/375ºF and spray the basket and the tops of the crab cakes with cooking spray. Place the crab cakes into the basket in a single layer. Cook until deep golden brown and crisp, about 12-14 minutes, flipping halfway through.
4. Meanwhile, make tartar sauce: Combine all of the tartar sauce ingredients in a bowl.
5. Serve the crab cakes warm with hot sauce, lemon wedges, and tartar sauce.

Extra Crispy Popcorn Shrimp

Servings: 2

Ingredients:

- 300g Frozen popcorn shrimp
- 1 tsp cayenne pepper
- Salt and pepper for seasoning

Directions:

1. Preheat the air fryer to 220ºC
2. Place the shrimp inside the air fryer and cook for 6 minutes, giving them a shake at the halfway point
3. Remove and season with salt and pepper, and the cayenne to your liking

Vegetarian & Vegan Recipes

Spring Ratatouille

Servings:2

Cooking Time:15 Minutes

Ingredients:

- 1 tbsp olive oil
- 4 Roma tomatoes, sliced
- 2 cloves garlic, minced
- 1 courgette, cut into chunks
- 1 red pepper and 1 yellow pepper, cut into chunks
- 2 tbsp mixed herbs
- 1 tbsp vinegar

Directions:

1. Preheat the air fryer to 190 °C / 370 °F and line the air fryer with parchment paper or grease it with olive oil.
2. Place all of the ingredients into a large mixing bowl and mix until fully combined.
3. Transfer the vegetables into the lined air fryer basket, close the lid, and cook for 15 minutes until the vegetables have softened.

Whole Sweet Potatoes

Servings: 4
Cooking Time: X

Ingredients:

- 4 medium sweet potatoes
- 1 tablespoon olive oil
- 1 teaspoon salt
- toppings of your choice

Directions:

1. Preheat the air-fryer to 200°C/400°F.
2. Wash and remove any imperfections from the skin of the sweet potatoes, then rub the potatoes with the olive oil and salt.
3. Add the sweet potatoes to the preheated air-fryer and air-fry for up to 40 minutes (the cooking time depends on the size of the potatoes). Remove as soon as they are soft when pierced. Slice open and serve with your choice of toppings.
4. VARIATION: WHOLE JACKET POTATOES
5. Regular baking potatoes can be air-fried in the same way, but will require a cooking time of 45–60 minutes, depending on their size.

Buffalo Cauliflower Bites

Servings: 4

Ingredients:

- 3 tbsp ketchup
- 2 tbsp hot sauce
- 1 large egg white
- 200g panko bread crumbs
- 400g cauliflower
- ¼ tsp black pepper
- Cooking spray
- 40g sour cream
- 40g blue cheese
- 1 garlic clove, grated
- 1 tsp red wine vinegar

Directions:

1. Whisk together ketchup, hot sauce and egg white
2. Place the breadcrumbs in another bowl
3. Dip the cauliflower in the sauce then in the breadcrumbs
4. Coat with cooking spray
5. Place in the air fryer and cook at 160°C for about 20 minutes until crispy
6. Mix remaining ingredients together and serve as a dip

Air Fryer Onions

Servings: 4
Cooking Time: 15 Mints
Ingredients:

- 1 white onion
- 1 tablespoon of oil
- 1/8 teaspoon of white suga

Directions:

1. Chop off both ends of your onion and peel away the skin.
2. Cut the onion in half.
3. Slice each half into semi-circle shapes, around 1/2 cm thick.
4. Lightly dress the onions with oil. Don't add the sugar yet.
5. Lay the onions in the air fryer basket, or underneath if you're cooking other items at the same time.
6. Cook at 150°C/300°F for 6 minutes, stirring halfway through.
7. Add the sugar and mix well to ensure all the onions have a little coating.
8. Cook at 150°C/300°F for another 8 minutes, stirring halfway through.

Tempura Veggies

Servings: 4
Ingredients:

- 150g flour
- ½ tsp salt
- ½ tsp pepper
- 2 eggs
- 2 tbsp cup water
- 100g avocado wedges
- 100g courgette slices
- 100g panko breadcrumbs
- 2 tsp oil
- 100g green beans
- 100g asparagus spears
- 100g red onion rings
- 100g pepper rings

Directions:

1. Mix together flour, salt and pepper. In another bowl mix eggs and water
2. Stir together panko crumbs and oil in a separate bowl
3. Dip vegetables in the flour mix, then egg and then the bread crumbs
4. Preheat the air fryer to 200ºC
5. Place in the air fryer and cook for about 10 minutes until golden brown

Air Fryer Stuffing Balls

Servings: 2
Cooking Time: 5 Mints
Ingredients:

- 1 slice of bread
- 1 medium onion
- 30 ml olive oil
- 30 g butter (unsalted)
- Handful of fresh sage or 1 tablespoon of dried sage

Directions:

1. Combine together the olive oil and butter in a wide based frying pan and heat until melted completely. Stir well.
2. Chop the onion and add this in.
3. Cook until translucent, usually 2-3 minutes.
4. Chop or roughly rip the bread and add this in. Stir well and cook for 1-2 minutes.
5. Chop the sage and add this in. Cook for 1 minute.
6. Stir well.
7. Place your mix into a food processor and pulse together until it's a fine consistency.
8. Roll into balls and then you can place the balls into your air fryer basket.
9. Cook in the air fryer at 200°C/400°F for 10 minutes. Shake halfway.
10. Serve and enjoy

Arancini

Servings: 12
Ingredients:

- 1 batch of risotto
- 100g panko breadcrumbs
- 1 tsp onion powder
- Salt and pepper
- 300ml warm marinara sauce

Directions:

1. Take ¼ cup risotto and form a rice ball
2. Mix the panko crumbs, onion powder, salt and pepper
3. Coat the risotto ball in the crumb mix
4. Place in the air fryer, spray with oil and cook at 200°C for 10 minutes
5. Serve with marinara sauce

Butternut Squash Fries

Servings: 2

Ingredients:

- 300g butternut squash, cut into sticks
- 1 tbsp olive oil
- 2 tsp bagel seasoning
- 1 tsp chopped rosemary

Directions:

1. Preheat air fryer to 200ºC
2. Drizzle oil over butternut squash and coat well
3. Add to air fryer and cook for about 20 minutes
4. Sprinkle with seasoning

Pakoras

Servings: 8

Ingredients:

- 200g chopped cauliflower
- 100g diced pepper
- 250g chickpea flour
- 30ml water
- ½ tsp cumin
- Cooking spray
- 1 onion, diced
- 1 tsp salt
- 1 garlic clove, minced
- 1 tsp curry powder
- 1 tsp coriander
- ½ tsp cayenne

Directions:

1. Preheat air fryer to 175ºC
2. Place all ingredients in a bowl and mix well
3. Spray cooking basket with oil
4. Spoon 2 tbsp of mix into the basket and flatten, continue until the basket is full
5. Cook for 8 minutes, turn then cook for a further 8 minutes

Artichoke Pasta

Servings: 2

Ingredients:

- 100g pasta
- 50g basil leaves
- 6 artichoke hearts
- 2 tbsp pumpkin seeds
- 2 tbsp lemon juice
- 1 clove garlic
- ½ tsp white miso paste
- 1 can chickpeas
- 1 tsp olive oil

Directions:

1. Place the chickpeas in the air fryer and cook at 200ºC for 12 minutes
2. Cook the pasta according to packet instructions
3. Add the remaining ingredients to a food processor and blend
4. Add the pasta to a bowl and spoon over the pesto mix
5. Serve and top with roasted chickpeas

Flat Mushroom Pizzas

Servings: 1

Ingredients:

- 2 portobello mushrooms, cleaned and stalk removed
- 6 mozzarella balls
- 1 teaspoon olive oil
- PIZZA SAUCE
- 100 g/3½ oz. passata/strained tomatoes
- 1 teaspoon dried oregano
- ¼ teaspoon garlic salt

Directions:

1. Preheat the air-fryer to 180ºC/350ºF.
2. Mix the ingredients for the pizza sauce together in a small bowl. Fill each upturned portobello mushroom with sauce, then top each with three mozzarella balls and drizzle the olive oil over.
3. Add the mushrooms to the preheated air-fryer and air-fry for 8 minutes. Serve immediately.

Vegetarian Air Fryer Kimchi Bun

Servings: 4
Cooking Time: 20 Mints
Ingredients:

- 1300 g pack of Quorn Mince
- 1/2 cup chopped kimchi, save a splash of kimchi juice
- 2-3 chopped spring onions
- 1 egg
- 1 tbsp sesame oil
- 1 tbsp soy sauce
- 1 tsp white pepper powder
- Pinch of salt
- For the dough:
- 480 g flour
- 260 ml warm water
- 2 g salt

Directions:

1. Combine all the dough ingredients in a large bowl, mix well and shape into a ball. Let the dough rest for 10 minutes before kneading for 5 minutes and then resting for a further hour.
2. Mix all the remaining ingredients together, ensuring all liquid has been well absorbed by the Quorn Mince.
3. Lay out the dough on a lightly floured surface and cut into 16 equal pieces (about 30g/piece).
4. Wrap an equal amount of filling into each piece of dough, using your hands to form into a smooth and tightly wrapped bun.
5. Preheat air fryer to 180°C/350°F Place the buns into the air fryer and spray some oil over the top of each bun, cook for 10-15 mins until golden and enjoy!

Miso Mushrooms On Sourdough Toast

Servings: 1
Ingredients:

- 1 teaspoon miso paste
- 1 teaspoon oil, such as avocado or coconut (melted)
- 1 teaspoon soy sauce
- 80 g/3 oz. chestnut mushrooms, sliced 5 mm/½ in. thick
- 1 large slice sourdough bread
- 2 teaspoons butter or plant-based spread
- a little freshly chopped flat-leaf parsley, to serve

Directions:

1. Preheat the air-fryer to 200°C/400°F.
2. In a small bowl or ramekin mix together the miso paste, oil and soy sauce.
3. Place the mushrooms in a small shallow gratin dish that fits inside your air-fryer. Add the sauce to the mushrooms and mix together. Place the gratin dish in the preheated air-fryer and air-fry for 6–7 minutes, stirring once during cooking.
4. With 4 minutes left to cook, add the bread to the air-fryer and turn over at 2 minutes whilst giving the mushrooms a final stir.
5. Once cooked, butter the toast and serve the mushrooms on top, scattered with chopped parsley.

Camembert & Soldiers

Servings: 2

Ingredients:

- 1 piece of Camembert
- 2 slices sandwich bread
- 1 tbsp mustard

Directions:

1. Preheat the air fryer to 180°C
2. Place the camembert in a sturdy container, cook in the air fryer for 15 minutes
3. Toast the bread and cut into soldiers
4. Serve with the mustard by the side

Air Fryer Frozen Veggie Tots

Servings: 4

Cooking Time: 8 Mints

Ingredients:

- 396 g Frozen Veggie Tots
- salt, to taste
- black pepper, to taste

Directions:

1. Place the frozen veggie tots in the air fryer basket and spread out evenly. No oil spray is needed.
2. Air Fry at 400°F/205°C for 5-8 minutes. Shake and gently stir about halfway through cooking. If cooking larger batches, or if your veggie tots don't cook evenly, try turning them multiple times on following batches.
3. If needed air fry at 400°F/205°C for an additional 1-3 minutes or until crisped to your liking. Season with salt & pepper, if desired

Saganaki

Servings: 2

Ingredients:

- 200 g/7 oz. kefalotyri or manouri cheese, sliced into wedges 1 cm/½ in. thick
- 2 tablespoons plain/all-purpose flour
- olive oil, for drizzling

Directions:

1. Preheat the air-fryer to 200°C/400°F.
2. Dip each wedge of cheese in the flour, then tap off any excess. Drizzle olive oil onto both sides of the cheese slices
3. Add the cheese to the preheated air-fryer and air-fry for 3 minutes. Remove from the air-fryer and serve.

Jackfruit Taquitos

Servings: 2

Ingredients:

- 1 large Jackfruit
- 250g red beans
- 100g pico de gallo sauce
- 50ml water
- 2 tbsp water
- 4 wheat tortillas
- Olive oil spray

Directions:

1. Place the jackfruit, red beans, sauce and water in a saucepan
2. Bring to the boil and simmer for 25 minutes
3. Preheat the air fryer to 185°C
4. Mash the jackfruit mixture, add ¼ cup of the mix to each tortilla and roll up tightly
5. Spray with olive oil and place in the air fryer
6. Cook for 8 minutes

Ravioli Air Fryer Style

Servings: 4

Ingredients:

- Half a pack of frozen ravioli
- 200g Italian breadcrumbs
- 200ml buttermilk
- 5 tbsp marinara sauce
- 1 tbsp olive oil

Directions:

1. Preheat the air fryer to 220°C
2. Place the buttermilk in a bowl
3. Add the breadcrumbs to another bowl
4. Take each piece of ravioli and dip it first into the buttermilk and then into the breadcrumbs, coating evenly
5. Add the ravioli to the air fryer and cook for 7 minutes, adding a small amount of oil at the halfway point
6. Serve with the marinara sauce on the side

Patatas Bravas

Servings: 4
Cooking Time: X

Ingredients:

- 750 g/1 lb. 10 oz. baby new potatoes
- 1 tablespoon olive oil
- ¼ teaspoon salt
- freshly chopped flat-leaf parsley, to garnish
- SAUCE
- 1 tablespoon olive oil
- 1 small red onion, finely diced
- 2–3 garlic cloves, crushed
- 1 tablespoon smoked paprika
- ¼ teaspoon cayenne pepper
- 400-g/14-oz. can chopped tomatoes
- 4 pitted green olives, halved
- ½ teaspoon salt

Directions:

1. Preheat the air-fryer to 200°C/400°F.
2. Rinse the potatoes and chop them to the same size as the smallest potato, then toss in the olive oil and sprinkle with the salt. Place the potatoes in the preheated air-fryer and air-fry for 18 minutes. Toss or shake the potatoes in the drawer halfway through.
3. While the potatoes are cooking, make the sauce. Heat the olive oil in a saucepan over a medium heat. Add the onion and sauté for about 5 minutes. Add the garlic, paprika and cayenne and cook for 1 minute. Add the tomatoes, olives and salt, plus 125 ml/½ cup water and simmer for about 20 minutes, until thickened. Purée the sauce in a blender or food processor.
4. Serve the potatoes in a bowl with the sauce poured over and the chopped parsley scattered over the top.

Air Fryer Chipotle Peppers And Gnocchi

Servings: 2
Cooking Time: 20 Mints
Ingredients:

- 1 tbsp chipotle paste
- 1 tbsp olive oil
- 1 lime, cut in half
- 250g/9oz goocchi
- 1 red pepper, seeds removed and cut into chunks
- 1 orange or yellow pepper, seeds removed and cut into chunks
- 1 small red onion, cut into chunks
- salt

Directions:

1. In a large mixing bowl, whisk together the chipotle paste, olive oil and the juice of one half of the lime to make a paste.
2. Toss the gnocchi, peppers, onion and a generous seasoning of salt in the mixture until everything is well coated. Tip into the air fryer.
3. Air-fry for 15–20 minutes at 200°C/400°F, stirring every 5 minutes with a spatula to make sure none of the peppers are sticking to the bottom and everything cooks evenly.
4. Serve topped with the avocado, soured cream and tomato salsa. Cut the remaining lime half into wedges and serve alongside

Air Fryer Vegan Fried Rice With Quorn Vegan Fillets

Servings: 2
Cooking Time: 20 Mints
Ingredients:

- 2 Quon Vegan Fillets, defrosted and sliced
- 325 g cold cooked rice
- 5 tbsp soy sauce
- 225g frozen vegetables (we used frozen edamame, peas, carrots and sweetcorn)
- 100 g firm tofu, crumbled (optional)
- 1 tsp sesame oil
- 1 tsp vegetable oil
- 2 green spring onions, chopped
- Salt to taste

Directions:

1. Place cold rice into a large bowl, combine with frozen vegetables, tofu (if using) and Quorn Vegan Fillets and mix.
2. Add the soy sauce and oil to the bowl. Mix until well combined.
3. Line Air Fryer with baking paper, pour in the rice ingredients, select air fry, set temperature to 180°C and set time to 15 minutes. Start/Stop your air fryer three times throughout the cooking time to stir.
4. Remove rice from the air fryer and sprinkle over chopped spring onions.

Side Dishes Recipes

Sweet And Sticky Parsnips And Carrots

Servings:2
Cooking Time:15 Minutes
Ingredients:

- 4 large carrots, peeled and chopped into long chunks
- 4 large parsnips, peeled and chopped into long chunks
- 1 tbsp olive oil
- 2 tbsp honey
- 1 tsp dried mixed herbs

Directions:

1. Preheat the air fryer to 150 °C / 300 °F and line the bottom of the basket with parchment paper.
2. Place the chopped carrots and parsnips in a large bowl and drizzle over the olive oil and honey. Sprinkle in some black pepper to taste and toss well to fully coat the vegetables.
3. Transfer the coated vegetables into the air fryer basket and shut the lid. Cook for 20 minutes until the carrots and parsnips and cooked and crispy.
4. Serve as a side with your dinner.

Cheesy Broccoli

Servings:4
Cooking Time:5 Minutes
Ingredients:

- 1 large broccoli head, broken into florets
- 4 tbsp soft cheese
- 1 tsp black pepper
- 50 g / 3.5 oz cheddar cheese, grated

Directions:

1. Preheat the air fryer to 150 °C / 300 °F and line the mesh basket with parchment paper or grease it with olive oil.
2. Wash and drain the broccoli florets and place in a bowl and stir in the soft cheese and black pepper to fully coat all of the florets.
3. Transfer the broccoli to the air fryer basket and sprinkle the cheddar cheese on top. Close the lid and cook for 5-7 minutes until the broccoli has softened and the cheese has melted.
4. Serve as a side dish to your favourite meal.

Ranch-style Potatoes

Servings: 2

Ingredients:

- 300g baby potatoes, washed
- 1 tbsp olive oil
- 3 tbsp dry ranch seasoning

Directions:

1. Preheat the air fryer to 220°C
2. Cut the potatoes in half
3. Take a mixing bowl and combine the olive oil with the ranch seasoning
4. Add the potatoes to the bowl and toss to coat
5. Cook for 15 minutes, shaking halfway through

Garlic And Parsley Potatoes

Servings: 4

Ingredients:

- 500g baby potatoes, cut into quarters
- 1 tbsp oil
- 1 tsp salt
- ½ tsp garlic powder
- ½ tsp dried parsley

Directions:

1. Preheat air fryer to 175°C
2. Combine potatoes and oil in a bowl
3. Add remaining ingredients and mix
4. Add to the air fryer and cook for about 25 minutes until golden brown, turning halfway through

Roasted Okra

Servings: 1

Ingredients:

- 300g Okra, ends trimmed and pods sliced
- 1 tsp olive oil
- ¼ tsp salt
- ⅛ tsp pepper

Directions:

1. Preheat the air fryer to 175ºC
2. Combine all ingredients in a bowl and stir gently
3. Place in the air fryer and cook for 5 minutes, shake and cook for another 5 minutes

Pumpkin Fries

Servings: 4

Ingredients:

- 1 small pumpkin, seeds removed and peeled, cut into half inch slices
- 2 tsp olive oil
- 1 tsp garlic powder
- 1/2 tsp paprika
- A pinch of salt

Directions:

1. Take a large bowl and add the slices of pumpkin
2. Add the oil and all the seasonings. Toss to coat well
3. Place in the air fryer
4. Cook at 280ºC for 15 minutes, until the chips are tender, shaking at the halfway point

Mexican Rice

Servings: 4

Ingredients:

- 500g long grain rice
- 3 tbsp olive oil
- 60ml water
- 1 tsp chilli powder
- 1/4 tsp cumin
- 2 tbsp tomato paste
- 1/2 tsp garlic powder
- 1tsp red pepper flakes
- 1 chopped onion
- 500ml chicken stock
- Half a small jalapeño pepper with seeds out, chopped
- Salt for seasoning

Directions:

1. Add the water and tomato paste and combine, placing to one side
2. Take a baking pan and add a little oil
3. Wash the rice and add to the baking pan
4. Add the chicken stock, tomato paste, jalapeños, onions, and the rest of the olive oil, and combine
5. Place aluminium foil over the top and place in your air fryer
6. Cook at 220°C for 50 minutes
7. Keep checking the rice as it cooks, as the liquid should be absorbing

Stuffing Filled Pumpkin

Servings: 2

Ingredients:

- 1/2 small pumpkin
- 1 diced parsnip
- 1 sweet potato, diced
- 1 diced onion
- 2 tsp dried mixed herbs
- 50g peas
- 1 carrot, diced
- 1 egg
- 2 minced garlic cloves

Directions:

1. Remove the seeds from the pumpkin
2. Combine all the other ingredients in a bowl
3. Stuff the pumpkin
4. Preheat the air fryer to 175°C
5. Place the pumpkin in the air fryer and cook for about 30 minutes

76

Zingy Roasted Carrots

Servings: 4

Ingredients:

- 500g carrots
- 1 tsp olive oil
- 1 tsp cayenne pepper
- Salt and pepper for seasoning

Directions:

1. Peel the carrots and cut them into chunks, around 2" in size
2. Preheat your air fryer to 220°C
3. Add the carrots to a bowl with the olive oil and cayenne and toss to coat
4. Place in the fryer and cook for 15 minutes, giving them a stir halfway through
5. Season before serving

Ricotta Stuffed Aubergine

Servings: 2

Ingredients:

- 1 aubergine
- 150g ricotta cheese
- 75g Parmesan cheese, plus an extra 75g for the breading
- 1 tsp garlic powder
- 3 tbsp parsley
- 1 egg, plus an extra 2 eggs for the breading
- 300g pork rind crumbs
- 2 tsp Italian seasoning

Directions:

1. Cut the aubergine into rounds, about 1/2" in thickness
2. Line a baking sheet with parchment and arrange the rounds on top, sprinkling with salt
3. Place another sheet of parchment on top and place something heavy on top to get rid of excess water
4. Leave for 30 minutes
5. Take a bowl and combine the egg, ricotta, 75g Parmesan and parsley, until smooth
6. Remove the parchment from the aubergine and wipe off the salt
7. Take a tablespoon of the ricotta mixture and place on top of each round of aubergine, spreading with a knife
8. Place in the freezer for a while to set
9. Take a bowl and add the two eggs, the pork rinds, parmesan and seasonings, and combine
10. Remove the aubergine from the freezer and coat each one in the mixture completely
11. Place back in the freezer for 45 minutes
12. Cook in the air fryer for 8 minutes at 250°C

Asparagus Fries

Servings: 2

Ingredients:

- 1 egg
- 1 tsp honey
- 100g panko bread crumbs
- Pinch of cayenne pepper
- 100g grated parmesan
- 12 asparagus spears
- 75g mustard
- 75g Greek yogurt

Directions:

1. Preheat air fryer to 200°C
2. Combine egg and honey in a bowl, mix panko crumbs and parmesan on a plate
3. Coat each asparagus in egg then in the bread crumbs
4. Place in the air fryer and cook for about 6 mins
5. Mix the remaining ingredients in a bowl and serve as a dipping sauce

Super Easy Fries

Servings: 2

Ingredients:

- 500g potatoes cut into ½ inch sticks
- 1 tsp olive oil
- ¼ tsp salt
- ¼ tsp pepper

Directions:

1. Place the potatoes in a bowl cover with water and allow to soak for 30 minutes
2. Spread the butter onto one side of the bread slices
3. Pat dry with paper, drizzle with oil and toss to coat
4. Place in the air fryer and cook at 200°C for about 15 minutes, keep tossing through cooking time
5. Sprinkle with salt and pepper

Bbq Beetroot Crisps

Servings:4
Cooking Time:5 Minutes
Ingredients:

- 400 g / 14 oz beetroot, sliced
- 2 tbsp olive oil
- 1 tbsp BBQ seasoning
- ½ tsp black pepper

Directions:

1. Preheat the air fryer to 180 °C / 350 °F and line the bottom of the basket with parchment paper.
2. Place the beetroot slices in a large bowl. Add the olive oil, BBQ seasoning, and black pepper, and toss to coat the beetroot slices on both sides.
3. Place the beetroot slices in the air fryer and cook for 5 minutes until hot and crispy.

Air Fryer Eggy Bread

Servings:2
Cooking Time:5-7 Minutes
Ingredients:

- 4 slices white bread
- 4 eggs, beaten
- 1 tsp black pepper
- 1 tsp dried chives

Directions:

1. Preheat your air fryer to 150 °C / 300 °F and line the bottom of the basket with parchment paper.
2. Whisk the eggs in a large mixing bowl and soak each slice of bread until fully coated.
3. Transfer the eggy bread to the preheated air fryer and cook for 5-7 minutes until the eggs are set and the bread is crispy.
4. Serve hot with a sprinkle of black pepper and chives on top.

Courgette Chips

Servings: 4

Ingredients:

- 250g panko bread crumbs
- 100g grated parmesan
- 1 medium courgette, thinly sliced
- 1 egg beaten

Directions:

1. Preheat the air fryer to 175ºC
2. Combine the breadcrumbs and parmesan
3. Dip the courgette into the egg then coat in bread crumbs
4. Spray with cooking spray and cook in the air fryer for 10 minutes
5. Turnover with tongs and cook for a further 2 minutes

Homemade Croquettes

Servings:4

Cooking Time:15 Minutes

Ingredients:

- 400 g / 14 oz white rice, uncooked
- 1 onion, sliced
- 2 cloves garlic, finely sliced
- 2 eggs, beaten
- 50 g / 3.5 oz parmesan cheese, grated
- 1 tsp salt
- 1 tsp black pepper
- 50 g / 3.5 oz breadcrumbs
- 1 tsp dried oregano

Directions:

1. In a large mixing bowl, combine the white rice, onion slices, garlic cloves slices, one beaten egg, parmesan cheese, and a sprinkle of salt and pepper.
2. Whisk the second egg in a separate bowl and place the breadcrumbs into another bowl.
3. Shape the mixture into 12 even croquettes and roll evenly in the egg, followed by the breadcrumbs.
4. Preheat the air fryer to 190 °C / 375 °F and line the bottom of the basket with parchment paper.
5. Place the croquettes in the lined air fryer basket and cook for 15 minutes, turning halfway through, until crispy and golden. Enjoy while hot as a side to your main dish.

Sweet Potato Wedges

Servings:4
Cooking Time:20 Minutes
Ingredients:

- ½ tsp garlic powder
- ½ tsp cumin
- ½ tsp smoked paprika
- ½ tsp cayenne pepper
- ½ tsp salt
- ½ tsp black pepper
- 1 tsp dried chives
- 4 tbsp olive oil
- 3 large sweet potatoes, cut into wedges

Directions:

1. Preheat the air fryer to 180 °C / 350 °F and line the bottom of the basket with parchment paper.
2. In a bowl, mix the garlic powder, cumin, smoked paprika, cayenne pepper, salt, black pepper, and dried chives until combined.
3. Whisk in the olive oil and coat the sweet potato wedges in the spicy oil mixture.
4. Transfer the coated sweet potatoes to the air fryer and close the lid. Cook for 20 minutes until cooked and crispy. Serve hot as a side with your main meal.

Corn On The Cob

Servings: 4
Ingredients:

- 75g mayo
- 2 tsp grated cheese
- 1 tsp lime juice
- ¼ tsp chilli powder
- 2 ears of corn, cut into 4

Directions:

1. Heat the air fryer to 200ºC
2. Mix the mayo, cheese lime juice and chilli powder in a bowl
3. Cover the corn in the mayo mix
4. Place in the air fryer and cook for 8 minutes

Potato Wedges With Rosemary

Servings: 2

Ingredients:

- 2 potatoes, sliced into wedges
- 1 tbsp olive oil
- 2 tsp seasoned salt
- 2 tbsp chopped rosemary

Directions:

1. Preheat air fryer to 190°C
2. Drizzle potatoes with oil, mix in salt and rosemary
3. Place in the air fryer and cook for 20 minutes turning halfway

Potato Hay

Servings: 4

Ingredients:

- 2 potatoes
- 1 tbsp oil
- Salt and pepper to taste

Directions:

1. Cut the potatoes into spirals
2. Soak in a bowl of water for 20 minutes, drain and pat dry
3. Add oil, salt and pepper and mix well to coat
4. Preheat air fryer to 180°C
5. Add potatoes to air fryer and cook for 5 minutes, toss then cook for another 12 until golden brown

Onion Rings

Servings: 4

Ingredients:

- 200g flour
- 75g cornstarch
- 2 tsp baking powder
- 1 tsp salt
- 2 pinches of paprika
- 1 large onion, cut into rings
- 1 egg
- 1 cup milk
- 200g breadcrumbs
- 2 pinches garlic powder

Directions:

1. Stir flour, salt, starch and baking powder together in a bowl
2. Dip onion rings into the flour mix to coat
3. Whisk the egg and milk into the flour mix, dip in the onion rings
4. Dip the onion rings into the bread crumbs
5. Heat the air fryer to 200°C
6. Place the onion rings in the air fryer and cook for 2-3 minutes until golden brown
7. Sprinkle with paprika and garlic powder to serve

Desserts Recipes

Grilled Ginger & Coconut Pineapple Rings

Servings: 4

Ingredients:

- 1 medium pineapple
- coconut oil, melted
- 1½ teaspoons coconut sugar
- ½ teaspoon ground ginger
- coconut or vanilla yogurt, to serve

Directions:

1. Preheat the air-fryer to 180°C/350°F.
2. Peel and core the pineapple, then slice into 4 thick rings.
3. Mix together the melted coconut oil with the sugar and ginger in a small bowl. Using a pastry brush, paint this mixture all over the pineapple rings, including the sides of the rings.
4. Add the rings to the preheated air-fryer and air-fry for 20 minutes. Check after 18 minutes as pineapple sizes vary and your rings may be perfectly cooked already. You'll know they are ready when they're golden in colour and a fork can easily be inserted with very little resistance
5. Serve warm with a generous spoonful of yogurt.

Lava Cakes

Servings: 4

Ingredients:

- 1 ½ tbsp self raising flour
- 3 ½ tbsp sugar
- 150g butter
- 150g dark chocolate, chopped
- 2 eggs

Directions:

1. Preheat the air fryer to 175ºC
2. Grease 4 ramekin dishes
3. Melt chocolate and butter in the microwave for about 3 minutes
4. Whisk the eggs and sugar together until pale and frothy
5. Pour melted chocolate into the eggs and stir in the flour
6. Fill the ramekins ¾ full, place in the air fryer and cook for 10 minutes

Cinnamon Bites

Servings: 8

Ingredients:

- 200g flour
- 200g whole wheat flour
- 2 tbsp sugar
- 1 tsp baking powder
- ¼ tsp cinnamon
- 3 tbsp water
- ¼ tsp salt
- 4 tbsp butter
- 25ml milk
- Cooking spray
- 350g powdered sugar

Directions:

1. Mix together flour, sugar, baking powder and salt in a bowl
2. Add the butter and mix well
3. Add the milk and mix to form a dough
4. Knead until dough is smooth, cut into 16 pieces
5. Roll each piece into a small ball
6. Coat the air fryer with cooking spray and heat to 175ºC
7. Add the balls to the air fryer and cook for 12 minutes
8. Mix the powdered sugar and water together, decorate

Sugar Dough Dippers

Servings: 12

Ingredients:

- 300g bread dough
- 75g melted butter
- 100g sugar
- 200ml double cream
- 200g semi sweet chocolate
- 2 tbsp amaretto

Directions:

1. Roll the dough into 2 15inch logs, cut each one into 20 slices. Cut each slice in half and twist together 2-3 times. Brush with melted butter and sprinkle with sugar
2. Preheat the air fryer to 150ºC
3. Place dough in the air fryer and cook for 5 minutes, turnover and cook for a further 3 minutes
4. Place the cream in a pan and bring to simmer over a medium heat, place the chocolate chips in a bowl and pour over the cream
5. Mix until the chocolate is melted then stir in the amaretto
6. Serve the dough dippers with the chocolate dip

Chocolate Orange Fondant

Servings: 4

Ingredients:

- 2 tbsp self raising flour
- 4 tbsp caster sugar
- 115g dark chocolate
- 115g butter
- 1 medium orange rind and juice
- 2 eggs

Directions:

1. Preheat the air fryer to 180ºC and grease 4 ramekins
2. Place the chocolate and butter in a glass dish and melt over a pan of hot water, stir until the texture is creamy
3. Beat the eggs and sugar together until pale and fluffy
4. Add the orange and egg mix to the chocolate and mix
5. Stir in the flour until fully mixed together
6. Put the mix into the ramekins, place in the air fryer and cook for 12 minutes. Leave to stand for 2 minutes before serving

Strawberry Danish

Servings: 2

Ingredients:

- 1 tube crescent roll dough
- 200g cream cheese
- 25g strawberry jam
- 50g diced strawberries
- 225g powdered sugar
- 2-3 tbsp cream

Directions:

1. Roll out the dough
2. Spread the cream cheese over the dough, cover in jam
3. Sprinkle with strawberries
4. Roll the dough up from the short side and pinch to seal
5. Line the air fryer with parchment paper and spray with cooking spray
6. Place the dough in the air fryer and cook at 175ºC for 20 minutes
7. Mix the cream with the powdered sugar and drizzle on top once cooked

Lemon Pies

Servings: 6

Ingredients:

- 1 pack of pastry
- 1 egg beaten
- 200g lemon curd
- 225g powdered sugar
- ½ lemon

Directions:

1. Preheat the air fryer to 180ºC
2. Cut out 6 circles from the pastry using a cookie cutter
3. Add 1 tbsp of lemon curd to each circle, brush the edges with egg and fold over
4. Press around the edges of the dough with a fork to seal
5. Brush the pies with the egg and cook in the air fryer for 10 minutes
6. Mix the lemon juice with the powdered sugar to make the icing and drizzle on the cooked pies

Chocolate-glazed Banana Slices

Servings:2
Cooking Time:10 Minutes

Ingredients:

- 2 bananas
- 1 tbsp honey
- 1 tbsp chocolate spread, melted
- 2 tbsp milk chocolate chips

Directions:

1. Preheat the air fryer to 180 °C / 350 °F. Remove the mesh basket from the machine and line it with parchment paper.
2. Cut the two bananas into even slices and place them in the lined air fryer basket.
3. In a small bowl, mix the honey and melted chocolate spread. Use a brush to glaze the banana slices. Carefully press the milk chocolate chips into the banana slices enough so that they won't fall out when you transfer the bananas into the air fryer.
4. Carefully slide the mesh basket into the air fryer, close the lid, and cook for 10 minutes until the bananas are hot and the choc chips have melted.
5. Enjoy the banana slices on their own or with a side of ice cream.

Chonut Holes

Servings: 12

Ingredients:

- 225g flour
- 75g sugar
- 1 tsp baking powder
- ¼ tsp cinnamon
- 2 tbsp sugar
- ½ tsp salt
- 2 tbsp aquafaba
- 1 tbsp melted coconut oil
- 75ml soy milk
- 2 tsp cinnamon

Directions:

1. In a bowl mix the flour, ¼ cup sugar, baking powder, ¼ tsp cinnamon and salt
2. Add the aquafaba, coconut oil and soy milk mix well
3. In another bowl mix 2 tsp cinnamon and 2 tbsp sugar
4. Line the air fryer with parchment paper
5. Divide the dough into 12 pieces and dredge with the cinnamon sugar mix
6. Place in the air fryer at 185ºC and cook for 6-8 minutes, don't shake them

Fruit Crumble

Servings: 2

Ingredients:

- 1 diced apple
- 75g frozen blackberries
- 25g brown rice flour
- 2 tbsp sugar
- ½ tsp cinnamon
- 2 tbsp butter

Directions:

1. Preheat air fryer to 150ºC
2. Mix apple and blackberries in an air fryer safe baking pan
3. In a bowl mix the flour, sugar, cinnamon and butter, spoon over the fruit
4. Cook for 15 minutes

Pumpkin Spiced Bread Pudding

Servings: 2

Ingredients:

- 175g heavy cream
- 500g pumpkin puree
- 30ml milk
- 25g sugar
- 1 large egg, plus one extra yolk
- ⅛ tsp salt
- ½ tsp pumpkin spice
- 500g cubed crusty bread
- 4 tbsp butter

Directions:

1. Place all of the ingredients apart from the bread and butter into a bowl and mix.
2. Add the bread and melted butter to the bowl and mix well
3. Heat the air fryer to 175ºC
4. Pour the mix into a baking tin and cook in the air fryer for 35-40 minutes
5. Serve with maple cream

Shortbread Cookies

Servings: 2

Ingredients:

- 250g flour
- 75g sugar
- 175g butter
- 1 tbsp vanilla essence
- Chocolate buttons for decoration

Directions:

1. Preheat air fryer to 180ºC
2. Place all ingredients apart from the chocolate into a bowl and rub together
3. Form into dough and roll out. Cut into heart shapes using a cookie cutter
4. Place in the air fryer and cook for 10 minutes
5. Place the chocolate buttons onto the shortbread and cook for another 10 minutes at 160ºC

Oat-covered Banana Fritters

Servings: 4

Ingredients:

- 3 tablespoons plain/all-purpose flour (gluten-free if you wish)
- 1 egg, beaten
- 90 g/3 oz. oatcakes (gluten-free if you wish) or oat-based cookies, crushed to a crumb consistency
- 1½ teaspoons ground cinnamon
- 1 tablespoon unrefined sugar
- 4 bananas, peeled

Directions:

1. Preheat the air-fryer to 180ºC/350ºF.
2. Set up three bowls – one with flour, one with beaten egg and the other with the oatcake crumb, cinnamon and sugar mixed together. Coat the bananas in flour, then in egg, then in the crumb mixture.
3. Add the bananas to the preheated air-fryer and air-fry for 10 minutes. Serve warm.

Chocolate Soufflé

Servings: 2

Ingredients:

- 150g semi sweet chocolate, chopped
- ¼ cup butter
- 2 eggs, separated
- 3 tbsp sugar
- ½ tsp vanilla extract
- 2 tbsp flour
- Icing sugar
- Whipped cream to serve

Directions:

1. Butter and sugar 2 small ramekins
2. Melt the chocolate and butter together
3. In another bowl beat the egg yolks, add the sugar and vanilla beat well
4. Drizzle in the chocolate mix well, add the flour and mix well
5. Preheat the air fryer to 165ºC
6. Whisk the egg whites to soft peaks, gently fold into the chocolate mix a little at a time
7. Add the mix to ramekins and place in the air fryer. Cook for about 14 minutes
8. Dust with icing sugar, serve with whipped cream

Breakfast Muffins

Servings:4

Ingredients:

- 1 eating apple, cored and grated
- 40 g/2 heaped tablespoons maple syrup
- 40 ml/3 tablespoons oil (avocado, olive or coconut), plus extra for greasing
- 1 egg
- 40 ml/3 tablespoons milk (plant-based if you wish)
- 90 g/scant ¾ cup brown rice flour
- 50 g/½ cup ground almonds
- ¾ teaspoon ground cinnamon
- ⅛ teaspoon ground cloves
- ¼ teaspoon salt
- 1 teaspoon baking powder
- Greek or plant-based yogurt and fresh fruit, to serve

Directions:

1. In a bowl mix the grated apple, maple syrup, oil, egg and milk. In another bowl mix the rice flour, ground almonds, cinnamon, cloves, salt and baking powder. Combine the wet ingredients with the dry, mixing until there are no visible patches of the flour mixture left. Grease 4 ramekins and divide the batter equally between them.
2. Preheat the air-fryer to 160ºC/325ºF.
3. Add the ramekins to the preheated air-fryer and air-fry for 12 minutes. Check the muffins are cooked by inserting a cocktail stick/toothpick into the middle of one of the muffins. If it comes out clean, the muffins are ready; if not, cook for a further couple of minutes.
4. Allow to cool in the ramekins, then remove and serve with your choice of yogurt and fresh fruit.

Apple Crumble

Servings: 4

Ingredients:

- 2 apples (each roughly 175 g/6 oz.), cored and chopped into 2-cm/¾-in cubes
- 3 tablespoons unrefined sugar
- 100 g/1 cup jumbo rolled oats/old-fashioned oats
- 40 g/heaped ¼ cup flour (gluten-free if you wish)
- 1 heaped teaspoon ground cinnamon
- 70 g/scant ⅓ cup cold butter, chopped into small cubes

Directions:

1. Preheat the air-fryer to 180°C/350°F.
2. Scatter the apple pieces in a baking dish that fits your air-fryer, then sprinkle over 1 tablespoon sugar. Add the baking dish to the preheated air-fryer and air-fry for 5 minutes.
3. Meanwhile, in a bowl mix together the oats, flour, remaining sugar and cold butter. Use your fingertips to bring the crumble topping together.
4. Remove the baking dish from the air-fryer and spoon the crumble topping over the partially cooked apple. Return the baking dish to the air dryer and air-fry for a further 10 minutes. Serve warm or cold.

Apple And Cinnamon Puff Pastry Pies

Servings:8

Cooking Time:20 Minutes

Ingredients:

- 4 tbsp butter
- 4 tbsp white sugar
- 2 tbsp brown sugar
- 1 tsp cinnamon
- 1 tsp nutmeg
- 1 tsp salt
- 4 apples, peeled and diced
- 2 large sheets puff pastry
- 1 egg

Directions:

1. Preheat the air fryer to 180 °C / 350 °F. Remove the mesh basket from the machine and line it with parchment paper.
2. In a bowl, whisk together the butter, white sugar, brown sugar, cinnamon, nutmeg, and salt.
3. Place the apples in a heatproof baking dish and coat them in the butter and sugar mixture. Transfer to the air fryer and cook for 10 minutes.
4. Meanwhile, roll out the pastry on a clean, floured surface. Cut the sheets into 8 equal parts.
5. Once the apples are hot and softened, evenly spread the mixture between the pastry sheets. Fold the sheets over to cover the apple and gently press the edges using a fork or your fingers to seal the mixture in.
6. Beat the egg in a bowl and use a brush to coat the top of each pastry sheet.
7. Carefully transfer the filled pastry sheets to the prepared air fryer basket, close the lid, and cook for 10 minutes until the pastry is golden and crispy.

Chocolate Souffle

Servings:2
Cooking Time:15 Minutes

Ingredients:

- 2 eggs
- 4 tbsp brown sugar
- 1 tsp vanilla extract
- 4 tbsp butter, melted
- 4 tbsp milk chocolate chips
- 4 tbsp flour

Directions:

1. Preheat the air fryer to 180 °C / 350 °F. Remove the mesh basket from the machine and line it with parchment paper.
2. Separate the egg whites from the egg yolks and place them in two separate bowls.
3. Beat the yolks together with the brown sugar, vanilla extract, melted butter, milk chocolate chips, and flour in a bowl. It should form a smooth, consistent mixture.
4. Whisk the egg whites until they form stiff peaks. In batches, fold the egg whites into the chocolate mixture.
5. Divide the batter evenly between two souffle dishes and place them in the lined air fryer basket.
6. Cook the souffle dishes for 15 minutes until hot and set.

Chocolate Dipped Biscuits

Servings: 6

Ingredients:

- 225g self raising flour
- 100g sugar
- 100g butter
- 50g milk chocolate
- 1 egg beaten
- 1 tsp vanilla essence

Directions:

1. Add the flour, butter and sugar to a bowl and rub together
2. Add the egg and vanilla, mix to form a dough
3. Split the dough into 6 and form into balls
4. Place in the air fryer cook at 180ºC for 15 minutes
5. Melt the chocolate, dip the cooked biscuits into the chocolate and half cover

Peanut Butter & Chocolate Baked Oats

Servings:9

Ingredients:

- 150 g/1 heaped cup rolled oats/quick-cooking oats
- 50 g/⅓ cup dark chocolate chips or buttons
- 300 ml/1¼ cups milk or plant-based milk
- 50 g/3½ tablespoons Greek or plant-based yogurt
- 1 tablespoon runny honey or maple syrup
- ½ teaspoon ground cinnamon or ground ginger
- 65 g/scant ⅓ cup smooth peanut butter

Directions:

1. Stir all the ingredients together in a bowl, then transfer to a baking dish that fits your air-fryer drawer.
2. Preheat the air-fryer to 180ºC/350ºF.
3. Add the baking dish to the preheated air-fryer and air-fry for 10 minutes. Remove from the air-fryer and serve hot, cut into 9 squares.

Strawberry Lemonade Pop Tarts

Servings: 12

Ingredients:

- 300g whole wheat flour
- 225g white flour
- ¼ tsp salt
- 2 tbsp light brown sugar
- 300g icing sugar
- 2 tbsp lemon juice
- Zest of 1 lemon
- 150g cold coconut oil
- 1 tsp vanilla extract
- 75ml ice cold water
- Strawberry Jam
- 1 tsp melted coconut oil
- ¼ tsp vanilla extract
- Sprinkles

Directions:

1. In a bowl mix the flours, salt and sugar. Mix in the cold coconut oil
2. Add 1 tsp vanilla and 1 tbsp at a time of the ice cold water, mix until a dough is formed
3. Take the dough and roll out thinly on a floured surface. Cut into 5cm by 7cm rectangles
4. Place a tsp of jam in the centre of half the rectangles, wet the edges place another rectangle on the top and seal
5. Place in the air fryer and cook at 200ºC for 10 minutes. Allow to cool
6. Mix the icing sugar, coconut oil, lemon juice and lemon zest in a bowl. Mix well. Top the pop tarts and add sprinkles to serve

Recipe Index

A

B

Printed in Great Britain
by Amazon

29804432R00057